THE ART OF THE PIVOT

THE ART OF THE PIVOT

DERRON PAYNE

NEW DEGREE PRESS

THE ART OF THE PIVOT

ISBN   978-1-64137-220-6   *Paperback*

           978-1-64137-221-3   *Ebook*

CONTENTS

DEDICATION

———

Dear Mama,

I'm dedicating this book to you, because if it weren't for you, I wouldn't be in the position that I am in today. I'm a published author now, Ma—who would've thought I'd get to this point? If there's one person who has always believed in me, it's definitely you. You have always been on my side.

Thank you for the unconditional love; for loving me even though there may have been times when I felt I didn't deserve it. Thank you for always being there to pick me up when I was at my lowest points. Thank you for teaching me kindness. Thank you for never turning your back on me. Thank you for always trusting me. Thank you for being the first person to show me what love was. Thank you for always being my #1 fan. Thank you for teaching me what my own self-worth was. Thank you for believing in me even when I didn't believe in myself. Thank you for being my mom.

Growing up watching you showed me my first example of a strong black woman and how you all are true superheroes. I've seen you do the impossible; even when we didn't have a lot, you made it work, Mom, and for that I will always be grateful. We never had a ton of money, but one thing we always did have was a ton of love. Even with our limited funds, you still showed me and Dani what a vacation and getting away for a little bit were.

Through all of my struggles, you are the reason I am mentally and emotionally okay today. I always had a problem opening up, and you are the reason I am getting better at it.

You are the reason I will always treat women with love and respect. You are the reason I am in the position I am today. You are the reason for all my progress. I know I give you a hard time for always putting everyone else before yourself, but it is the reason why I want to always help people. You are the reason I want to have a positive impact on the world.

Mom, I want you to know that your struggles do not go unnoticed and I appreciate you for enduring all of it, because if you didn't—there would be no me.

Ma, you were recently diagnosed with breast cancer. I didn't tell you this at first because I was trying to remain strong for you, but I did not take it very well. I was scared at the thought of possibly losing my superhero. After thinking and processing it, I realized how hard this must be on you, but I want to let you know that we will get through this. We have been hit with adversity before, and we have never let it get the best of us so there is no reason to stop now. You are going to fight and I am going to be at your side the entire time. We are going to beat cancer.

I love you, Mom.

TRIBUTE TO VICTOR VIVIAN RICHARDSON

————

Rest in Peace Mr. V

You passed away a week before this book was sent to layout, and I didn't know how to feel at first, I wanted you to be there on launch day, especially after being there for me for most of my life, but at least now your name will live on forever.

You were one of the strongest people I knew , you've had a very influential role in my life for the past 9 years.

I want to thank you for everything that you did for my mom, everything that you have done for my sister, and everything you have done for me. You were definitely some of the closest family that I had in some very important years of my life. Thank you for always having my back.

From our long talks about sports or all of the advice you have given me over the years, I appreciated all of it. You've given me great examples of what it means to be a man, and take care of your family. You were the only person I know that would get mad when I tried to pay you back.

It was sad to see you go, but the fact that you are no longer in pain puts a smile on my face through the tears because you didn't deserve that.

You are finally at peace looking down on us and playing cards everyday, and that puts me at peace.

Thank you for being the person you were, you will never be forgotten.

INTRODUCTION

———

(From Webster Dictionary)[1]

pivot

noun

piv·ot | \ ˈpi-vət \

———

1   "Definition Of PIVOT". 2019. *Merriam-Webster.Com*. https://www.
merriam-webster.com/dictionary/pivot.

DEFINITION OF *PIVOT* (ENTRY 1 OF 3)

1: a shaft or pin on which something turns **2a:** a person, thing, or factor having a major or central role, function, or effect **b:** a key player or position *specifically* : an offensive position of a basketball player standing usually with back to the basket to relay passes, shoot, or provide a screen for teammates **3:** the action of pivoting *especially* : the action in basketball of stepping with one foot while keeping the other foot at its point of contact with the floor

pivot

adjective

DEFINITION OF *PIVOT* (ENTRY 2 OF 3)

1: turning on or as if on a pivot **2:** PIVOTAL

pivot

verb

pivoted; pivoting; pivots

DEFINITION OF *PIVOT* (ENTRY 3 OF 3)

intransitive verb
: to turn on or as if on a pivot

transitive verb
1: to provide with, mount on, or attach by a pivot
2: to cause to pivot

* * *

When you think of the word pivot, you probably think of all or at least one of the definitions above. Growing up I heard that word a lot, but only ever in the context of basketball. At first it was a difficult term for me to grasp, but to be fair to myself, I heard the term for the first time as a seven-year-old basketball player and most of my teammates had a hard time understanding it too. Even when I actually did figure out the pivot, I didn't truly appreciate it in its entirety until I was a bit older.

Fast-forward a few more years…

It was a warm spring night in the year 2010, and I was on my eighth-grade trip, a cruise from New York to the Bahamas. (My classmates were all enjoying the great adventures one could experience on a Norwegian cruise ship.) Yet I was where any basketball fan would be at the time: sitting in front of a television screen watching the 2010 NBA finals. It was a matchup between the Los Angeles Lakers and the Boston Celtics, a legendary rivalry that had been going on for years. I was originally watching the game with a few friends but after they finished their food they left to explore the ship some more. But not me. This game was going down in basketball history.

There were so many future Hall of Famers on the court at once; I was in a basketball fan's paradise. What more could you ask for? With all of these great players on the floor, you would be surprised at which player had one of the most defining plays of the game for me—the point guard of the Celtics.

He stood at about the half-court line, with his defender not too far in front of him, blocking his path to the basket. He orchestrated a play that would have his two front-court guys, aka the two biggest players on his team, set a double on ball screen at the top of the key better known as the three-point line. The play was basically the two guys using their bodies to shield the point guard from his defender so he could proceed to the basket. It seemed like a foolproof plan, but just as the point guard saw his clear path to the basket, the biggest defender on the opposing team switched his attention to him. As the point guard got all the way to the basket, he was met by a seven-foot brick wall—the only thing standing between him and the basket. The point guard, standing at just 6′4″, seemed powerless, as if he were all out of options. All I could think about was that he was in such an impossible position: not only was he met at the basket by a seven-footer, but he had also picked up his dribble, which meant he could no longer move. Just as I thought all hope was lost, I witnessed one of the most beautiful moves in the game of basketball. He planted his left foot into the ground, almost as if he had placed his foot on a sticky glue trap. He then swung his right leg around and rotated his body, resembling a ballerina in the process of a big spin. It happened so fast, but it kept replaying back in my head in slow motion. He was going at full speed and in the midst of an obstacle getting in his way, he pivoted, leading to his success of two points from scoring the basket.

Now, I didn't tell that story to bore you with the details about a cool basketball game, but rather to share with you the beauty of the move. I wanted to share how the move—the pivot—is not just a move that you make when you feel like there's nowhere to go, but it also can be. Not just in basketball, but in life in general. That's the point of this book. The hours of writing that I put in are all for this one end goal of helping someone who might be in the same position I was in, or a similar one. Writing this book was one of the hardest things I have ever done—not just because it was a lot of words being put on a page, but because the topic is something close to my heart, something I have actually experienced. In order to help people in similar situations, I had to be open, and *vulnerable*. Something I had struggled with in the past, maybe because of where I grew up or who I was around. But it is something I have begun to feel more comfortable with now. There were times when reliving some of these stories brought me to tears, but feeling that raw is what helped me lay out the best takeaways for each situation and story. Pivoting is something that should never be limited to only one story; for that reason, I also spent time researching the pivot of a few key people and compiling their stories into this book.

I feel like I was only able to make my pivot after getting mentors who shared information with me that I previously hadn't had access to. I honestly feel like I was just put in the right places at the right time and met the right people who wanted to help me. My pivot would have never been a thought if it hadn't been for some key lessons I learned along the way. So now my goal is to share these lessons with all of you.

Throughout this book, I will leave helpful takeaways, for you, in the form of PIVOT points: actionable pieces of advice you can implement in your life now.

PREPARE

CHAPTER 1

ART OF SELF-AWARENESS

———

The universe has no restrictions. You place restrictions on the universe with your expectations.

—DEEPAK CHOPRA

* * *

"Wait, he has a gun!" screamed a random person.

Pop! Pop! Pop! Three gunshots had rung out, and it was as if the entire world froze for a second.

My fifteen-year-old self snapped back to reality, as a rush of people began scrambling to safety. It was instinctual as I dashed from the basketball court, not thinking of anything else but getting to safety. It would've helped if I actually knew where the shooting came from. Amid my original desire to flee the scene, I noticed I had forgotten something: my house keys. They were right where I had left them; on the side of the court, wrapped inside of a shirt, inside of a small drawstring bag. I immediately turned around and proceeded to the court to retrieve it.

What was I doing? What was I thinking? I knew this was a bad idea, but why couldn't I stop my legs from moving toward the court? This decision might have been one of the stupidest I'd ever made. How would my mother feel knowing that I was not only hurt—or worse, dead—because I decided to go back into the danger zone?

I arrived back at the court, which was, by that time, completely empty. It was the most unlikely sight in a New York City park on a warm summer day. As I bent down and picked up my keys, I got this strange feeling within me. It was like when you feel eyes on you, causing you to return the look, almost like a burning sensation that you can't resist. I began to feel wary of the situation, because who could be staring at me on a deserted court after a shooting? Except…the shooter.

When I finally looked up, I froze. This was one moment in my life when I did not feel anything. A lot of people say they have experiences of their life flashing before their eyes when faced with a life-or-death situation. But that was not what happened to me in this moment. Thoughts of me growing up. Thoughts of my friends and family. Thoughts of what the future could possibly hold for myself. I was not thinking of any of this; not one of these thoughts popped into my head. Not even once. My mind was completely empty. Blank. This was a new feeling. I had just made eye contact with the potential perpetrator. Though I didn't see the weapon, it felt as though I could lose my life in an instant. This stare seemed to last for a lifetime, when in reality it was only a measly few seconds. He looked right at me, almost like he was looking through me, then he turned away and back in the direction of his enemy, almost as if his brain immediately processed that I wasn't it.

This was no random stranger though. This was a familiar face—not a friendly one, but definitely familiar. I had seen him many times in the park. I had actually witnessed him rob people and get into altercations on separate occasions. Now that I'm thinking about it, he never actually bothered me. Every time we saw each other in the park or around town it was just a head nod or a fist bump. I never hung out with him; we were not friends—more like passing acquaintances.

Many stories of this guy had floated around the neighborhood, but the only lesson I got from them was that you should just stay away. These were not good stories in any way, shape, or form. They mostly involved violence and bullying. He was a pretty big guy, definitely a six-footer, and he had a pretty wide frame. Generally a guy whose bad side you would not want to be on, although from the stories I've heard, you didn't have to do much to be in the pathway of his wrath. I am fairly certain this guy was in his early to mid-twenties, and he had just casually robbed some of the teenagers in the park who were around my age.

This guy for some reason never bothered me, and—not that I was complaining or anything—I was curious as to what made me different from other people similar to me in age. Why was I not targeted? What made me so special? Did he consider me special? Well, I do not know if he considered me special, but he definitely did consider me different. Everytime I would play pick-up in the park against the adults, my game seemed a lot more advanced than the other kids my age in the park—which is why the adults would even let me play with them in the first place. As time went on, I went from being a kid playing with the adults to being that kid they wanted on their team. I believe this man noticed as well. I believe he also noticed my work ethic and how I would actually work out before pick-up. I can only recall one encounter with this man that involved words, which was him asking where I played high school ball and whether I wanted to go pro. I remember telling him that I played for Benjamin Banneker Academy (a public high school in Brooklyn, NY) and I also played for a couple AAU teams. I remember his response clearly—it's actually my most vivid memory of him: "You have to make it for the hood." Was that why he always left me alone? There were tons of talented players in NYC but not necessarily in my neighborhood. Did basketball save my life?

* * *

As I began to write this story, I struggled a lot—not with brainstorming ideas, but with determining what I actually felt comfortable sharing. This story was one of the first I wrote, and one of the only ones that I wrote straight through until the end. Even though it was one of my original stories, it was not one I thought would actually make it into the book. It took a lot of self-reflection and deep thinking. Telling this story and a few other stories that I have included in later chapters is my way of letting the world inside of my head. For me, letting anyone know how I felt has long been an internal struggle. It could have been the result of many different factors surrounding me growing up. But this was going to be a little different: this wouldn't be opening up to a friend or to family, which I already struggled with. This would be opening up to the world. When I reevaluated why I was writing this book and who I was writing it for, I realized that for it to be a resource used to help people, I had to share real and honest stories. I don't want your sympathy but rather for you to think deeply about the details in all of the stories I share with you.

Did basketball save my life? Perhaps. But did that mean I now owed my entire life to the game of basketball? Maybe one dangerous situation doesn't warrant such a drastic suggestion, but what if there was another?

* * *

THE GAME WITH THE WAGER

It was another normal summer day for me, sometime when I was in high school, and I decided to go to the park. Going to the park to play ball was a normal thing for me. Either I would go all day or, if I had practice or a game, I would just go to the park after. Gym memberships in New York City are ridiculously expensive and I just couldn't afford one, so the park is where I would reside. Now, I had two systems for when I would go to the park. The first was, if I was going to the park after practice or a game, I would just be going to play pick-up games with the adults and/or the kids who were good enough to play with. The second was, if I didn't have practice or a game I would get to the park early and work out on my own before proceeding to play pick-up games. Either way you look at it, I was getting some games in, probably because of my super competitive nature.

This was a day that I didn't have any practice or games, so I decided to go to the park early to work out before the pick-up games. About halfway through my workout I was approached by a local teen in neighborhood, who started to heckle me a bit. This kid wasn't very good, even though he thought he was, so I just ignored him for the most part. When he saw his heckling was not working, he proceeded to tell me how he was so much better than me at basketball. I found this rather amusing, so much so that I started to laugh right in his face, which he did not like very much.

"Play me one-on-one," he said in his most serious tone.

"No. One, because I'm working out, and two, because it's just not a fair game at all." This probably came across as too confident, and thinking back maybe I should've just responded with a simple no.

"What size do you wear? Let's play one-on-one for each other's shoes," he said with even more seriousness in his tone.

At this point, it was clear he was getting heated and I needed to figure out some way to resolve this before the situation became physical. It may seem far-fetched, but in the neighborhood I grew up in, it honestly did not take much for things to escalate. There were many issues that I would have to work around while trying to find a solution. For one, there was no way my pride would allow me to ever lose to him. I had immense respect for the game and believed that losing on purpose showed I had no heart. I also knew that if the game had a wager and I didn't collect the wager after winning, I would be looked at as "soft," and that definitely was not something you wanted for yourself in my neighborhood, simply because it made you an easy target. My solution was a little dangerous because it could be taken as disrespect, but I felt like it was my best option at the time: I offered to play him, but the wager was that if I won, I did not receive anything, and if he won he would get my shoes and basketball. He agreed to the terms.

We had a history of guarding each other. When the adults didn't have enough players for a full game, they would allow him to play, and of course they would make him guard me because we were close in age. He had a history of fouling hard when things were not going his way, and when playing against me it was a regular occurrence. I tried to play through the fouls as much as I could while at the park, because I felt like doing so made me tougher and because calling "foul" too much can lead to people getting agitated. Through these games, I think he felt as though we had developed a sort of rivalry and his anger came from me not acknowledging him as a rival. It was true; I did not see him as a rival but more like any other aggressive player who didn't like me very much. I believed our games were on two different levels—I worked out all the time and he did not work out at all. How could I ever see him as an equal on the basketball court? Even though I've always had this confidence on the court, I will admit that he did make me better, by forcing me to learn how to score through contact and be tougher.

I shot the ball to see who would get to have possession and I made the shot, which gave me the ball first. When the one-on-one game started, it was going relatively smoothly; I made my first couple of shots. To give a little bit more context on the game, winner gets the ball. That means if you score, the ball would be in your possession again. First person to get to eleven points wins the game. I had made my first five shots, which put me up: the score was five to zero. This is when the game started to get a little physical. I was maybe two inches taller than my opponent, but he was stocky and I'm pretty sure weighed more than me, so I was feeling all of the shoves and hits. I was accustomed to being fouled, so I played through it. After I scored a few more points, the adults swarmed into the park getting ready to play pick-up, and they asked if I was playing. I responded yes, just as soon as this game was over. The adults decided to wait for me so they stood around the side of the court and watched the game. I was now up ten to zero and he was determined that he would not let me score. I faked left and drove to the right side of the basket. He caught up to me and fouled me hard from behind. I did manage to get the shot off, though, and it went in, so I sat on the floor flexing my frail arms (at the time I was about fifteen and hadn't really started hitting the weights yet).

After the game came to its end, the adults swarmed the court, hyping me up because of the last play (but honestly I'm pretty sure they were just happy to get on the court and play a game now themselves). My opponent was not too pleased about this. Actually, he was furious, and getting more upset by the second. In the moment, I did not realize it. What made it worse was that the adults started to heckle him, and instead of directing any of his anger at them, he directed it all toward me. He slowly started approaching me and no one had realized yet.

"What's so funny?" he questioned with such fury in his voice.

"I honestly wasn't laughing—I usually have a smile on my face," I replied, maintaining my smile. Thinking back to this moment, I could see how provoking this could be, but I was fifteen and filled with a ton of pride.

"You think I'm playing with you?" he asked, getting closer.

"What?" I replied, not that I couldn't hear, but my sense of pride emerged, as I needed to show that he didn't scare me. I did not want a fight; I hated fighting, always have, and firmly believed it was for people who could not articulate themselves properly.

Just when I was thought, *How can I avoid this?* one of the adults grabbed him and pushed him away from me and told him to get out of the park.

> *"You've got a future, kid. Don't ruin it for someone like that!"*

—the adult who essentially saved me

I don't even remember his name, but he may have saved my life. I didn't know what to say, so I just nodded my head. Was it basketball that saved me?

* * *

Fights happened all the time in this neighborhood and at this park specifically. The park had a terrible reputation. Fights were such a natural occurrence that it was almost weird to see someone preemptively trying to stop one. Why me? What was different about me and every other young person around my age—that I was an above-average basketball player in the neighborhood? Well, whatever it was, basketball was definitely part of the reason. Everyone would tell me that basketball was my way out of where I was from. The sport kept me out of trouble and, as you can see, possibly even saved my life a few times. When you see all the events that took place, you start to believe that this sport might just be your lucky rabbit's foot. And that's how I felt—I couldn't possibly let it go. But what happens when society tells you the same thing?

∗ ∗ ∗

SOCIOLOGY OPENED MY EYES

It was my first semester in the honors program at Rockland Community College, technically. It was the fall semester after spending a summer abroad studying in Cambridge, England—I was admitted into the honors program in the spring semester, but it was midway through, so I didn't officially get to take honors classes yet. This was my first taste of what the honors college was like. In order to complete the program, you have to take eight honors courses. Because it was my last year at RCC, I had to fit these eight courses in my last two semesters (well, technically seven, because studying abroad at the University of Cambridge counted as an honors seminar). So I decided I would take three honors courses during the fall semester and four honors courses in the spring. The three I chose for the fall were macroeconomics, contemporary poetry, and sociology. I enjoyed all the courses that I took, but one in particular had more of an impact on me than the others: honors sociology. Credit could be due to the sociology professor, who was an amazing woman and teacher. Through our lessons she had real conversations with us—conversations I needed to hear, especially growing up as a minority in this country—and on top of it all, she truly cared about the well-being of each of us. I don't know if she realized this, but what may have seemed like an average class session for her would change my perspective forever.

It was an average day for me. I woke up at around 4:30 a.m. to begin my long commute to Rockland Community College to go to an early morning basketball practice. Practice started at 6 a.m. and usually consisted of conditioning and strength workouts. We typically had two practices a day, the second of which was at around 3:30 p.m. and included more skill, training, and going over plays. Between those two practice times, I attended class as I always did. There was nothing different from this day and any other day I spent at Rockland, or at least that's what I thought at the beginning of the day. It wasn't until honors sociology that all of that changed.

I walked into class and went straight for my seat, the middle seat in the second row (there were no assigned seats but it was like an unspoken rule to keep the same seat that you took on the first day of classes).

Dr. Padilla arrived and we began class. It seemed like it was going to be an interesting one when she told us what the lesson plan for the day was. We were going to be discussing socioeconomic class, a term I was not familiar with but had an idea what it might be about from context clues. I figured that it had something to do with wealth, that the wealthiest people would be in the highest socioeconomic class. As it would turn out, however, it's not that simple.

Dr. Padilla assumed we all knew that wealth was a factor, so she asked if anyone thought they knew what else was important when considering socioeconomic status.

"Influence is another important factor when considering socioeconomic class status."

—a random person in class

I sat back in my seat and pondered this idea of wealth and influence, during which time Dr. Padilla asked for examples of people we thought were in the highest class. My hand immediately shot into the air. I knew exactly who I would use:

"LeBron James! He is very wealthy and has a huge following," I said with such confidence, remembering the $1 billion life-time deal LeBron had just signed with Nike.

"That's a great guess, but not quite," Dr. Padilla replied.

"What do you mean?" I asked, slightly confused at this point.

"Well, Lebron won't really sit at the same table as the Rockerfellers, you know," she said.

And at first I didn't completely understand. I assumed it had to do with race, which is partially true but not the full picture. Seeing the perplexed look of everyone in the class, Dr. Padilla decided to give us some more clarity. She explained that there were three determining factors of socioeconomic class.

"Education, occupation, and wealth."

—Dr. Padilla

She also explained that the most important of the three was education for a couple of reasons. Higher education is the one place where all of the socioeconomic classes meet and interact together. Most people die in the same socioeconomic class status they were born into, but higher education gives you the opportunity to change that.

PIVOT Point #1 — Societal views don't have to define you.

Only (brother) up in first class, old lady tryna be friendly, ayy /
She think I'm in the NBA, why a (brother) can't have his MBA?
/ Next time I'ma flip the script, you know, kick some ish that's
gon' shock her / "You're so tall, what team do you play for?" /
No (lady), I'm a doctor.

—J. Cole[2]

This is a song lyric from the song "Chris Tucker" on the mix-tape "Truly Yours 2" by J. Cole, also known as Jermaine Cole. It really embodies how I feel I'm perceived by the world at times, primarily due to the media. In most scenarios or situations, I am always expected to be the most athletic. These assumptions are not solely placed on me or people like me, but on everyone. Society forces these expectations on you from birth, and if you aren't exposed to anything else, you may feel like these societal views are absolute.

You may not be able to change what you look like or where you come from, but embrace who you are. You are not limited to what society thinks you should be doing.

---

2   Cole, Jermaine. 2013. *Chris Tucker.* Mixtape. Dreamville Records.

PIVOT Point #2 — Just because something or someone saved you doesn't mean you owe them your life.

This pivot point gives us some insight on the very important topic of second chances. When we feel we have gotten lucky and received a second chance, we shouldn't waste it doing things that we don't want to do. Even if something or someone saved you, that doesn't mean you owe them your life (or else what was the point of them saving you?).

PIVOT Point #3 — Learn your "WHY?" and constantly refer back to it.

It is important to figure out *why* you are doing the things you do; it will help with your long-term success if you can keep referring back to it. Your "WHY?" can be anything—it just has to be important to you. It does not matter if you have been doing the same thing for your entire life; if your "WHY?" is no longer there, then it is time to move on to something new.

CHAPTER 2

SELF ASSESSMENT (HOW TO FIND OUT IF YOU'RE ON THE RIGHT PATH)

———

Your mind knows only some things. Your inner voice, your instinct, knows everything. If you listen to what you know instinctively, it will always lead you down the right path.

—HENRY WINKLER

* * *

FASHION TO FRAGRANCE

What happens when your dream job just isn't as fulfilling for you anymore?

Imagine going through your undergraduate years of college with a goal in mind. Imagine knowing everything you wanted to do while being so young. It would potentially make life a lot easier: you could take classes and choose a major tailored toward the career you wanted to pursue.

For Agnieszka Sygnarowicz Burnett, that was exactly the case—she had a dream to become a journalist and a writer, so she attended to journalism school. After finishing up in school, Burnett did what a lot of people can't and secured the job of her dreams at *Glamour Magazine*. For most people, getting a job at *Glamour* would be enough to sustain them, being at such a well established place, but Burnett said it best herself: *"I've never been one to follow the herd."*

Realizing that she was no longer fulfilled in her career like she had previously been, she decided to attend a post-baccalaureate science studies program at Columbia University, where she would meet her husband Benjamin in a physics class. After completing her studies, she and her husband co-founded Nomaterra Fragrances. Burnett explained the experience like this: *"We worked out of our tiny New York City apartment. I was the happiest I'd ever been. ... I trusted my nose to steer me in the right direction; I utilized my knowledge of chemistry, my experience in beauty, and my passion for nostalgic travel to create 'scentsory' experiences that transport one to a different time and place."*[3]

After the reevaluating her life, she realized this was more along the lines of what she wanted to be doing, in contrast to what her younger self thought she would want to do.

> *"It was the best decision, to make the leap from a traditional career path to one where we are in complete control of our company, its integrity and ethos."*

> —Burnett[4]

* * *

THE JANE DOZE DUO

The Jane Doze is an electric music DJ duo that is slowly but surely taking the world by storm. The duo consists of two

3   Brustein, Darrah. 2015. "9 Entrepreneurs Tell Their Stories Of Pivoting 180 Degrees To Start New Careers". *Entrepreneur*. https://www.entrepreneur.com/article/246965.
4   Brustein, Darrah. 2015. "9 Entrepreneurs Tell Their Stories Of Pivoting 180 Degrees To Start New Careers". *Entrepreneur*. https://www.entrepreneur.com/article/246965.

women, Jen Mozenter and Claire Schlissel, who at first glance may seem to be regular women but that couldn't be farther from the truth. They have performed at sold out shows all over the country and even shared a stage with world famous DJ, Diplo. The real surprise through all of this is that when they started they were both doing this part time while having full time office jobs in New York City. In an interview they talk a little about what this experience was like:

"We did this one show in Chicago that would never have worked unless we had the time difference. Jen left after work, flew to Chicago, and went directly to the club to play the set."[5] said Claire.

"Oh yeah, that was brutal," exclaims Mozenter. "I slept on a bench in the airport because I had to catch the first flight back to New York to go to work in the morning."

They even talked about this mysterious feeling it gave them until they got a little too popular. "At first it was cool-like a Batman lifestyle. A lot of people didn't know. But then we had a print feature in Billboard Magazine, and since I worked

5   Jong, Anneke. 2019. "Career Remix: Why The Jane Doze Quit Their Jobs To Take The Stage". *Themuse.Com*. https://www. themuse.com/advice/career-remix-why-the-jane-doze-quit-their-jobs-to-take-the-stage.

in the music industry, my co-workers saw it. They were like, 'Um, WTF?'" explained Jen.

Then things started to get a bit rocky when juggling their job became too much for them. Jen says, "It was really hard because I wanted to be 100% present for my day job and for my clients. It got to the point where we spent so much of our free time playing shows that we were running out of time to make the music to play at the shows. Quality can really suffer when you're balancing too many things."

At this point they decided that they had to make a choice, and they decided to go the Jane Doze way.

For Jen this was not the easiest task because she felt as though she had her dream job working in digital marketing at Columbia, she claims, "It was really hard for me to make this change. Working in the music industry was the path I always wanted. When I got the job, I fully immersed myself in the world of digital marketing, helping artists develop their voice online. I loved it. But this opportunity came up and it presented a choice between an awesome known path and a totally crazy unknown path as an artist. I picked the latter because the other path will always be there."

Claire decision making process went a bit differently, she said, "Until we start making our own music to sell, almost all of our income comes from gigs. I think we knew for a while that [doing The Jane Doze full time] was the goal, but we had to decide if we could actually pay our rents doing this. We looked back at the last six months and saw that we could have paid our rent, so that was encouraging. But some of it is faith. We had to believe that by putting in 100%, we could make it."

There are always a ton of things to fear about the unknown but a lot of time when you actually go through with the process those previous fears can feel trivial.

"My biggest fear about leaving my job was that I wouldn't be able to fill my days. I haven't even thought about that fear since I quit because I've been so busy." claimed Jen.

Happy and content with her choice Claire agreed, "I can't imagine what this month would have been like with a day job. Between making music, doing our shows, and coordinating everything for SXSW (South by Southwest Music Festival), it really is a full-time job."

PIVOT Point #4 - Re-evaluate your dreams, they may have changed

We are constantly growing and evolving, sometimes what we once thought we wanted forever changes, especially when we are making a lot of decisions at such a young age. It is important to constantly make sure your dreams are still your dreams, as we grow and learn we sometimes develop new dreams and it is important to not feel confined to older passions that you may have outgrown.

PIVOT Point #5 - Consider a change if you feel like a small fish in a huge sea

When you're put in a position where you feel like you are too small in a big place it may be time to consider a change. Being in a place like that limits growth and if you aren't learning or growing then it is time to move on.

PIVOT Point #6 - Check where you spend your free time

Evaluate your entire day, figure out how much time you spend on each task. Look at the tasks that aren't required and pay attention to how much time you're spending on tasks. If you're spending all of your free time on something it could be your passion, and you should check to see if there was anyway that you could turn this into a career.

ITERATE

CHAPTER 3

IMPOSTER SYNDROME

———

So I have to admit that today, even 12 years after graduation [from Harvard], I'm still insecure about my own worthiness. I have to remind myself today, "You are here for a reason." Today, I feel much like I did when I came to Harvard Yard as a freshman in 1999. ... I felt like there had been some mistake — that I wasn't smart enough to be in this company and that every time I opened my mouth I would have to prove I wasn't just a dumb actress. ... Sometimes your insecurities and your inexperience may lead you to embrace other people's expectations, standards, or values, but you can harness that inexperience to carve out your own path — one that is free of the burden of knowing how things are supposed to be, a path that is defined by its own particular set of reasons.

—NATALIE PORTMAN

*　*　*

I was in my second semester at Rockland Community College and things were starting to feel a little different. I was no longer only excited to go to school to attend basketball practice or to play in a basketball game. What was different now? I had changed my major and was now studying business. I was most excited to go to "Principles of Finance," not just because I really liked finance but also because of my professor in this class: Professor Repic. He became one of my first mentors. He actually worked in the field of finance and shared real-world experience with me. I was always really engaged because I had never heard stories like that before, and only saw glimpses of these types of lives on TV. At this point, basketball was still the most important thing to me but something else of importance was brewing inside me. Professor Repic's class might be what that single-handedly got me interested in school, and it was starting to show. Professors were noticing, and in classes I wasn't too fond of in the beginning I was now at the top. Among these was my English class, a subject I had dreaded ever since middle school, and now that professor was recommending me for the honors program.

*　*　*

THE NEWFOUND FOCUS

After switching my major and ending up a business student, I gained a newfound focus. Speaking to Professor Repic from my finance class almost daily let me know that there was more out there that I could achieve. It was really the awareness that woke me up; I never had the knowledge that someone like me could achieve some of the things that Professor Repic talked about. But he would never just talk about it—he would always give me a plan or show me a way to achieve these things. It didn't feel like it was unattainable when he was sharing with me. I had felt like success in general was in this locked box, and the only way I could obtain the golden key to open the box was through basketball. This professor showed me that there were multiple ways to the golden key, and one sure path was knowledge. That resonated and stuck with me.

* * *

MY LOVE/HATE RELATIONSHIP WITH ENGLISH MADE ME AN HONOR STUDENT

I'd hated English ever since I was a little kid, so what was different now? Did I really hate English or did I hate the boring way it was taught? I had to take "College Writing II" during the same semester I switched my major. For some reason I didn't hate it. Well, more than that, actually: I rose to being one of the top students in the class. But how? This was a class I had hated for my entire life. Could it be the change of major that just had me more focused in general, or was it this new teaching style that I wasn't familiar with? Or, could it simply be that the reading and writing assignments given in this class in particular were not given to make students fall asleep? It might've been the fact that we read exciting short stories and not long, drawn-out, boring novels. Whatever it was, I liked it. It felt good to be positively acknowledged by all my professors that semester.

One day in this English class, our professor came in and taught us for half of the class before saying she had some news to share with us. We all had a very good idea of what the news was: she was pregnant. But what did that mean for the class? Well, that we were getting a new professor in the middle of the semester. This abrupt change scared me for a couple of reasons, the first being that the new person might make me hate English again. What if her entire teaching style was totally different? What if she liked long novels? The second concern was about grading. How was she going to figure out grades? Would she have the same policies as our original professor? All were questions that I couldn't get answered until we received the new professor and experienced her teaching for ourselves. After our professor shared the news with us, she looked directly at me and said that she needed to see me after class. I was so confused—what could she want to see me for? Why me specifically? Why only me? Did I do something wrong? I guessed I would just have to wait and find out at the end of class.

So I stayed back after class. My professor waited for everyone to leave before beginning. She started out by telling me that I was one of the brightest students in her class, that she also taught honors courses and felt as though I belonged there. She told me there was absolutely no reason why I should not be in the honors program right now. I had never even heard of the honors program at Rockland Community College prior to this conversation with her. She then asked me if I was interested, and I didn't know what to say, but I did know that I liked getting positive attention for doing well in school—so I said yes. She said she would recommend me to the honors program and that all I would have to do was speak to either Hannah, the assistant director of the honors program, or Dr. Lynch, the head of the program. I told her I would do it. Then she looked me in my eyes and said, "Don't just say that—make sure you go to the office." I nodded, and that was that.

When I got home, I decided I would do some research on this honors program at Rockland Community College, which I had never heard about. After tons of searching on the web, I concluded that the program was legit. It had students transferring into almost all of the top schools in the country, and that's when I started to doubt myself. Did my English professor make a mistake? Would I really fit in the honors program? Their students were transferring to Ivy League and other top-tier universities every year. Where would I fit in a program like that? But I supposed I couldn't be recommended for no reason; maybe my English professor saw something in me, right? Still unsure of myself, I walked past the honors office every day for the next two weeks, each day telling myself that I would go in the next day. After those weeks passed, I finally decided to go in. I had walked past it plenty of times before, but walking *in* was different. Stepping into the office for the first time was intimidating. I felt a change in atmosphere, almost as if I didn't belong there. But I also didn't want to turn back. It was the first time I felt comfortable feeling uncomfortable. The first person I met was the assistant coordinator, Hannah. We discussed the possibility that I could dream bigger than I ever thought I could, by focusing on my studies instead of on basketball. She then told me that the requirement for being an honors student was a 3.5 GPA, and sadly, at the time I only had a 2.4. But for some reason, she didn't turn me away—she looked deep into my eyes and for a moment it felt as though she could see my past and my future; she saw me for more than just the numbers on the page. She believed in me when most people wouldn't even give me a second thought, and that meant the world to me.

Who would've thought that after that semester and taking one class in the first summer session my GPA would sky-rocket to a 3.4. After this I went back to the office to see Hannah and of course she wasn't surprised, she said she knew that I would do it. She then told me that she took a chance on another student a couple years before me, and that I reminded her of him a little bit. His name was Febin, you'll learn a bit more about him later in the book.

PIVOT Point #7 — Learn to Get Comfortable Feeling Uncomfortable

When doing new things for the first time it will always be a bit uncomfortable, sometimes it will be so uncomfortable that you may contemplate whether it's worth it or not. Do not let these feelings deter you from taking action, embrace these moments. Every uncomfortable moment I have experienced since pivoting has been worth it and now I look forward to them.

CHAPTER 4

THE ART OF SMALL CHANGES FIRST

———

While it may seem small, the ripple effects of small things is extraordinary.

—MATT BEVIN

* * *

CAMBRIDGE FOR THE SUMMER

"Wait, so I can study abroad while at community college?" I questioned with a puzzled face.

"Yes, you can, Derron—there is actually a wonderful opportunity for you through the honors program," answered Hannah.

"Really! What is it, exactly?"

"Well, you have the ability to study abroad at the University of Cambridge, in England, this summer. It's only a summer program, but it is very intensive and you will earn four honor credits."

I paused for a moment and the room fell silent. This would be the longest I had been away from my coaches, ever since I was nine years old. How would my game be affected? What about my conditioning? I needed to stay in shape for next season.

Then my thought process was interrupted by Hannah, who seemed to be confused by my blank expression.

"If you are interested, you need to let me know by tomorrow, because the deadline has technically already passed, being that we are halfway through the spring semester already."

Feeling like my chances of heading to England for the first time were slipping away, I quickly responded, "I am definitely interested in going," not knowing what that would entail.

"Okay, great, well—the trip is about $3000, which includes housing, breakfast, and dinner. But you would need to find and pay for a roundtrip flight, and also have a bit of change on you for anything extra you would like to do while there."

"I will definitely make it happen," I said, not knowing if it were true or not.

I left the honors office that day with so many mixed emotions. My entire drive home, I left the radio off, although it probably wouldn't even matter—my thoughts were so loud I could barely hear anything else.

Am I really going to do this? I had never been to Europe before. Could I pass up this opportunity? This was the University of Cambridge, one of the oldest and most prestigious universities in the world. There had to be a gym of some sort. If not, it would probably be one of the prettiest places for me to go running so I could stay in shape for basketball next season. During that car ride, I went from *Am I doing this?* to *How can I make this work?* Now that I had made up my mind came the real problem.

How am I going to pay for this? I guess the logical decision would've been to just tell my parents and get it from them. Right? Wrong. There were many things wrong with this scenario. For one, I was staying with my mom at the time, not just because it was easier to commute to Rockland Community College every day, but also because my father and I were not really on speaking terms. Growing up, he sometimes reminded me of the father from *Everyone Hates Chris*, a real penny pincher sometimes, so aside from my pride not allowing me to ask him, I doubted that he would've donated to the cause anyway. My mom, on the other hand, was the opposite. She would've gladly given me any amount of money I that I needed to go abroad—too bad she didn't have the money. We were already struggling; there was absolutely no way we could afford this trip if we were already living paycheck to paycheck. Either way, I still needed to figure something out, because I could not miss this opportunity.

Think, think, think... That's it! I know what to do. Ask grandma. Apart from her loving me and wanting the best for me, she was also the most financially disciplined person I knew. If there was anyone who had money saved and would be gladly willing to help me, it was her.

There's one thing that you need to know about my grandmother: although she is willing to help me with anything, her financial discipline would not allow her to spend money on anything foolish. So, that being said, I had to get all my information together and make my case. Now, I knew it wouldn't be too hard to convince her, as she is a huge fan of school and would do anything to see me at the best schools possible. In other words, the Cambridge name helped a lot. The only thing I really needed to do was get all my numbers together, so I did. That night I called my grandma with the most detailed proposal and elaborate plan on how we would succeed in making it work—and, yes, it did include me getting a job for the last two and a half months before the trip.

6 weeks later:

I stared down at 9:30 p.m. boarding pass as I was approaching John F. Kennedy airport in the backseat of the car. As my eyes bored into the pass, I could not hear or see anything around me. I was in a daze; I couldn't believe this was actually happening. Then it was like a switch went off in my head and I snapped back into reality: I was at the airport. I gave my family hugs and then was ready to set off on my new adventure, only to be stopped by a massive security line. But being so excited to go to Europe for the first time in my life, I could not complain about the line no matter how long it was. Once I cleared security, I realized that my flight was delayed by about an hour, so I just waited patiently, my excitement not allowing me to be upset or annoyed.

Upon entering the plane it occurred to me that this was the biggest aircraft I had ever been on. I walked through the large aisles for about five minutes until I found my seat. The best thing about my seat was that it was in the aisle, so I didn't face the risk of sitting between two bad travel companions—the most I could get was one. Next I read the menu, after which I thought I thought a pleasant meal was in store. When I received the meal, however, I understood why there are so many jokes about airline food. I had planned to fall asleep after my meal, but with so much excitement I could not. I found myself watching an entire three-hour movie and then half of another one before I could finally catch some shut-eye.

When I had finally arrived at my destination, Heathrow Airport, I was like a child in a toy store, eyes wide looking around at everything. I remember asking for directions to baggage claim even though I could read the signs, just so I could hear the English accent and make the situation feel even more real than it already felt. After I gathered my bags from baggage claim, I was greeted by family that I had never met before. My aunt Denise Parke (R.I.P to an amazing woman with a beautiful soul), her 2 children and her brother. They gave me a warm welcome to England and then we were off. After letting them know that I would be studying abroad in the UK they offered to pick up from the airport and take me to Cambridge, a near 2-hour drive. The first thing we did was stop for something to eat at a local KFC, it was interesting to see the change in the menu from the US KFC menu. After eating and talking for a bit we had set out for our long drive. At some point during the beginning of this journey the sleep finally caught up with me and I knocked out for the entire trip. My aunt woke me when we had arrived and all of a sudden any bit of sleepiness had disappeared, I was mesmerized by how beautiful the campus was, the University has 31 colleges and I was staying in Selwyn College. My family stayed with me until I received my credentials, found my room, and settled in. After this, they gave me hugs, we took a group picture, and then they set off to head home.

Now it was time for a new adventure, I had to head to the welcome ceremony. Sitting through it I was starting to realize just how powerful the program could be for me. After this, I headed to the dining hall for dinner. I was amazed at first glance at the dining hall, there were really long tables, raised ceilings, and had a real Harry Potter feel to it. The room was filled with students from all around the world, and everyone was curious about each other's cultures. At the time I was a pretty shy individual but I was also an extrovert, so basically I wanted to be around and talk to people but I was too shy to make the attempt to approach. Being in this room it was different, I was being approached by a ton of different people who were just curious and wanted to befriend me. This helped break me out of my shell, I realized that I was shy because I was afraid of the possibility of someone being mean, but most people were nice, and if they weren't I could just move on to the next.

Most students went out on the first couple of nights but I didn't, not because I didn't want to but because I pretty sick on the first two days. I still don't know why I was sick but I just assumed it was because of the change of environment and the jetlag. On the third day, I decided that I would not let being a little under the weather keep me from enjoying this experience. On this third day, we had an excursion/project, it was to this beautiful garden and we had to collect different species of insects. For this project, we had to get into groups of three. Most people found their groups pretty and to my surprise so did I, I was approached by these two girls, Caitlyn from Alabama and Sophie from Melbourne, two really cool people who still remain close friends of mine to this day. The project was successful and I had also found my partners in crime for the rest of the trip.

Aside from all of the fun that I had on this trip, academically it was very inspiring for me. I was doing a science program, more specifically I was studying conservation biology, something that had nothing to do with business which is what I'm currently studying in school. Regardless of that, I was very interested in every topic and lesson. Being in a room with so many smart students and all of these renowned professors helped me realize that I needed that experience again.

BACK IN THE STATES

I had just come back from what was at the time the best experience of my life. There were still a couple weeks left of summer, and I was on my way to work. This was a sales job I got to save money for the trip (Grandma wasn't going to give me everything). I was just happy that the company wanted me to come back after my study abroad experience because it was another opportunity for me to earn some extra cash before the new school semester started. One thing that was not so pleasant about this job was how far it was from my house, but I'll admit that the company was amazing about the reimbursement for gas so I didn't mind too much.

I was still in a trance from my experience in England, so much so that I could not even be a little annoyed at all of the morning traffic on my way to the job. My entire ride was filled with reminiscing and missing my time back there. Before I knew it, I had arrived at my work destination for the day; the hour-and-a-half commute felt more like just a half an hour. Also, to give a little bit more context on the sales representative job I had, I was a field rep, so I was at a different location almost every time I was on shift.

This day, I was at a farmers market somewhere in upstate New York. Farmers markets were a place I became all too familiar with; they were a place where the company usually did very well, primarily because its products were green. The typical population you find at farmers markets are people who care about the environment, so I enjoyed going to these locations too. That was where I usually made most of my sales. Although farmers markets were prime spots for me, there were the days when I got sent to markets in the middle of nowhere. Those days were very boring, but at least you had the company of your coworker to carry you along, unless of course you were scheduled to work by yourself. This workday in particular I had to deal with all of the problems listed above: I was scheduled to work at a market that felt deserted aside from the other vendors, and I was scheduled to work it alone.

On days like that, I was glad to have taken Professor Repic's "Principles of Finance" class and that he taught me not only the importance of reading but also how fun it could be, because that was all that I had to rely on for my entire five-hour shift. Or was it? After I was finished reading the Wall Street Journal, thanks again to Professor Repic encouraging the subscription, I continued reading a book from the *Rich Dad, Poor Dad* series. During this reading session, my phone started vibrating. I was usually not supposed to take calls during work unless it pertained to the job, but I figured that since no one was there it would be okay. After checking the caller ID and seeing it was Hannah, I thought I would be even more justified to answer the phone, seeing as it could be an important matter regarding school. I answered the phone excited to hear from her, seeing as I had not talked to her since coming back from Cambridge.

"Hi Derron, are you busy?" she asked.

"Hi Hannah! And nope—I am free to talk," I said, full of excitement, completely ignoring the fact that I was at work. I was so lucky it was a quiet day.

"So how was Cambridge?" she asked in a jolly tone, and I could just imagine the huge smile that must've been on her face.

Asking this question was like opening up a can of worms. *How do I respond? What do I say? A better question would've been: what do I not say?*

"It was the best experience of my entire life," I said, reliving all the great adventures I had just lived a couple weeks back. I began to tell her everything that happened during my study abroad experience and how it changed my perspective and thinking in a lot of cases.

MY FORMER INTENTIONS

When I first went to Rockland Community College, I had a clear idea of what I planned to do. I was always the type of person to strategically plan out everything I wanted to do, no matter what that was. So that was exactly what I did for basketball; Rockland Community College was only one piece of the puzzle for me. My plan was to go there, play for the team, lead it to a division championship, and then the next year to a conference championship. During this time, I planned to be going through the recruiting process, trying to get an athletic scholarship to a four-year institution to continue playing. I planned to be actively reaching out to coaches at different athletic programs while expecting to get some attention from others at invitational tournaments.

Things changed dramatically when I changed my major and entered those new business classes that spring semester. I no longer desired to attend just any school for basketball; I actually cared about what the academics were like at the school. Even though basketball was still the most important thing at a school for me, having a strong business program was now also important.

* * *

THE FRESH PRINCE[6]

Now I know you probably heard of Will Smith before, he is a world famous movie star. If you don't know him from his movies you definitely know him from his Instagram where he has over 33 million followers, and regularly posts funny content. What most people probably don't know is that Will started as a rapper and then by chance got a great opportunity to transition into acting. So how did he get to that point?

Will came out as a rapper with the stage name, The Fresh Prince. He performed as sort of a duo tag team with his boy DJ Jazzy Jeff as his DJ. They came out with their debut album "Rock the House" on March 19, 1987, and it did pretty well. Then a year later on March 29, 1988, they released the biggest album of their career, "He's the DJ, I'm the Rapper," it included their smash hit "Parents Just Don't Understand." Aside from increasing their bank accounts this album increased their fame and they were thrust into the spotlight. They won a Grammy and the album went triple platinum, it seemed as if they were on the top of the world, so they did what any newcomer to money and fame would do and they spent all of it. Will had cars and motorcycles.

---

6   Smith, Will. 2019. "How I Became The Fresh Prince Of Bel-Air | STORYTIME". *Youtube*. https://www.youtube.com/watch?v=y_WoOYybCro.

"I called the Gucci store in Atlanta, and I was like, 'will y'all close it down if I bring my friends?', and I'm smiling but that's stupid."

—Will Smith

But then they dropped another album and things seemed to go all downhill from there. The name of the album was "And in This Corner…" and according to Will:

"It was a tragedy it went like double plastic"

—Will Smith

Not to mention he was living a super luxurious lifestyle, and had already spent all of his money. This was a bad situation but what could make matters worse…The IRS and TAXES…

Will claims that it wasn't like he forgot it was just something that he really didn't pay attention to until the IRS came for their money. Since he spent all of that already, they took his cars and fancy toys.

"Being famous and broke is a (bad) combination"

—Will Smith

Around this time Will's girlfriend approached him for a rather serious conversation:

"Dude we're not doing this, like you're not just going to be laying around this house all day doing nothing," said Will's girlfriend.

Will answered, "What am I supposed to do?"

"Go where people is doing it," she said,

"Where people doing it?"

"Go to the Arsenio Hall show!"

"Just go stand around at the Arsenio Hall show?"

"YES!"

"That's stupid!"

But despite his disagreement with the idea, he went to the show anyway. There he met a man named Benny Medina, who at the time was the Vice President of A&R at Warner Bros.

Benny had an idea for a show featuring a teenage boy moving to live with his rich aunt in Beverly Hills to get away from trouble in his own neighborhood. He pitches the idea to Will. Will's thoughts were basically like cool but I'm not an actor. Benny then says he wants to introduce him to Quincy Jones, who would be producing the show with him.

At this time it's December 1989, about a year and half after Will's Grammy winning album dropped.

Will finds himself at Quincy's house and he is amazed at all of the notable people there at the time from actors to politicians. Benny introduces Will to Quincy and the conversation goes like this:

"Aye man, I saw your music videos I love what you're doing, tell me you rap name again"

"They call me The Fresh Prince"

"Alright good that's what we're going to call the show"

Quincy then handed Will the screenplay for "A Failed Morris Day" pilot and told him to take 10 minutes to study the script, he said that he was going to have the movers clear out the stuff out of the living room so that Will could audition.

"Aye Q, hold up man, hold up, I'm not ready to do no audition," said Will.

Quincy answered, "Alright, alright, well what do you need, tell me what you need,"

"Just set the meeting for a week and I could do it,"

"Yeah, yeah you Brandon Tartikoff the head of NBC is out there, I'll get him to schedule for next week, then you know what's going to happen, something is going to come up and he's going to have to reschedule."

"Oh yeah, so then like 3 weeks from now"

"Yeah, yeah, yeah, 3 weeks from now will be good, or you could take 10 minutes right and change your life forever."

"F*** it then, YES, give me 10 minutes!"

Will killed the audition and then the lawyers drew up the first deal for a show that we all may have heard of before, "The Fresh Prince of Bel Air."

Then they all took pictures and signed the deal, 3 months later they are filming the pilot.

PIVOT Point #8 — Put yourself out there.

You have to be willing to put yourself in positions to experience new things, show people that you are open to new opportunities. It may seem scary at times but don't be afraid to try.

PIVOT Point #9 — Do the little things; they can turn into big things.

When you are making a major change or pivot you have to start somewhere, the little changes are very important. They have the power to be a catalyst that leads to even bigger changes.

CHAPTER 5

SETBACKS

———

Never make a decision when you are upset, sad, jealous or in love.

—MARIO TEGUH

* * *

What happens when you're on a new path and there's a roadblock? Not something minor—I'm talking about a huge obstacle that causes things to change. When your back is against the wall, you'd be surprised at the decisions some people will make. When the pressure is on emotions, can cloud your judgment and cause you to do things you might not have otherwise. Well, this exact thing happened to me just when I began exploring the possibilities of pivoting. I was switching, then I almost dropped all of this to join the Navy.

* * *

Growing up in New York City, I was approached by different armed forces recruiters all the time, but it was never something I even considered. While I do have the utmost respect for those who serve, I never thought I would do the same. I mean, I didn't even really believe in fighting. In my view, the right words can solve almost anything—or at least I believe that *should* be true. The military was just something that I always believed wasn't for me.

So how did I get to this point, where I was ready to pull the trigger on something I previously wouldn't even consider?

At the time I was only an undergraduate student at Rockland Community College working on an associate's degree in the honors program. I was commuting to Suffern, NY, every day by car (about an hour drive unless during rush hour, when it was more like two hours). This was a drive I once dreaded, but when I started to undergo my pivot, I viewed it as part of my upward climb. I started listening to audiobooks, and it was great; I felt like I was learning so much. I was now excited to go to school, because I was curious and my mentors would keep feeding my curiosity. Whenever I learned anything new

I would come home eager to share with anyone who would listen—usually that would be my mother or my grandmother, who would FaceTime me from Trinidad.

But this all changed when I came home one day to my mother in tears. She didn't like crying in front of me or my sister, always trying to portray strength so we wouldn't worry. This time she could not hide it, though—the pain must've been too strong.

"I got laid off. I don't know what we're going to do!"

—my mother

I froze for a bit, because in this moment it was the first time she had dropped the facade that everything was going to be okay. Every time we had previously been in a tough situation, she would always assure me that we would get through it. This time I knew it just might be too much for her to handle alone. We had known that it might've been a possibility because the travel company that she was working for at the time needed to cut costs, so they started laying people off. They had three waves of firing before getting to her so we thought that she might be safe, until she got that phone call.

"Don't worry, Ma. We'll get through it; we always do!"

—my reply to her

After all the years of my mother being the superhero who saves the day, it was my turn to reassure her that we got this. But now I had to start brainstorming how we were actually going to get through this situation. We had bills to pay, not to mention we still had to eat.

I became so frustrated; I didn't know what to do. I needed money and I needed it now. My mother, who I was leaning on and lived with, had just lost her job, and what made it worse was that right before that we were living paycheck to paycheck, so there were no savings for a rainy day.

I thought about going to my father for help, but things weren't going well with our relationship at the time, so asking him wasn't an option. Typically, going to him for anything money-related wasn't a good idea unless I wanted to get my feelings hurt, but every now and then I would get lucky. However at this point in time we were not even on speaking terms (but that's a story for another day).

What other options did I have at this point?

I started to look around me and noticed a lot of people joining the armed forces (Army, Navy, Air Force, etc.). Looking even closer, I saw that my big cousin had joined the Navy. Seeing that for what it was and everything it came with it, I decided to do some further research online. If you know anything about the internet, once I started looking it up all I would see were ads for the Navy.

After one really bad day, I almost pulled the trigger on the decision of joining the Navy. It was after having car problems that day, and my mother's car was imperative when it came to getting to school every day, so we had to resolve the issue. Seeing that additional stress it put on my mother was too much for me. Later that night I grabbed my laptop and went to the Navy website, with tears in my eyes as I hovered my mouse over the "APPLY" button. The tears came from seeing my mother cry, thinking about the stress she was going through, and feeling like there was nothing that I could do to immediately stop it. Right before I was about to press the button, I decided to weigh the pros and cons of the situation.

After letting my emotions pass and thinking about it deeply with a clear mind, I realized that joining the Navy was not the right choice for me. It would have been a hasty decision that I would have later regretted. I liked the current path I was on and just had to find a way to make that work.

I ended up getting a part-time job on campus working twenty hours a week in the Student Involvement Office, as well as having my part-time sales job that I did over the summer.

Things were a little tougher on me for a few months, but it was better than giving up the life I wanted to live in the future.

PIVOT Point #10 — Beware of hasty decisions—they can be detrimental.

Growing up I always heard the saying "haste makes waste." I didn't understand it until I got older, but now I know it means that when you rush, you sometimes miss key details, which in turn can sometimes ruin whatever you are doing.

PIVOT Point #11 — Do a situation analysis before any decision.

Doing a situation analysis before decision-making allows you to see the move from every angle. You want to know what the strengths, weaknesses, opportunities, and threats are. This will help you take emotion out of the equation to ensure a more logical decision making process.

VALIDATE

CHAPTER 6

GATHERING INFORMATION

———

An investment in knowledge pays the best interest.

—BENJAMIN FRANKLIN

* * *

FOUNDING A BANK TO E-COMMERCE

Is it normal for one to change his career from banking to e-commerce?

Well, maybe not but that is what Jeff Chambers did, and he is anything but normal. This bank where Jeff previously worked was co-founded by him. It was called Alterra Bank, and it was primarily for helping tech based startups. They were very successful and a lot of that was because of their focus on technology and efficiency. He enjoyed what he did but decided that he would switch it up after they decided to sell the bank. He describes the experience like this:

"We started the bank with a clear strategy of staying focused on entrepreneur-led companies and distributing services through technology rather than brick-and-mortar branches. After we sold the bank, I knew my time in heavily regulated industries was over, but my desire to apply the same principle of 'clicks over bricks' didn't change."[7]

He got his next big idea from a company that came to his bank for funding. It was a company that sold radiators for large trucks. He noticed that 25 percent of their revenue came from internet sales, that fact was enough to capture his interest. He decided to investigate some more and through his research he found out that aftermarket parts for Class 4 to Class 8 trucks was a $20 billion industry, and only 1 percent of that comes from online sales. That's when he decided to change that and thus BigMachineParts.com was born.

7   Brustein, Darrah. 2015. "9 Entrepreneurs Tell Their Stories Of Pivoting 180 Degrees To Start New Careers". *Entrepreneur*. https://www.entrepreneur.com/article/246965.

Jeff explains how he felt jumping into this venture, all of his feelings, the outside factors, all of it:

"You always have that pit in your stomach – is this going to work? ... But you have to believe in yourself. You have to have confidence that you know, at least from a business strategy perspective, you're building the right thing, you've done the right due diligence and work...To jump into this, to literally write a check for everything I've got in order to make this happen, to go out and find an investor willing to believe in you and write a check on your behalf, that's a lot of responsibility. And I have a wife and three little girls, so you lay in bed at night, and you're like, 'What did I do?' But then you wake up in the morning, and it's like, 'I can't think of anything I'd rather do.' This is the most fun I've had in business up to this point."[8]

* * *

FINANCE TO RUM[9]

Now I'm not saying that finance always leads to alcohol, but for Bridget Firtle it certainly did, but not in the way you

---

8   Collins, Leslie. 2015. *Bizjournals.Com*. https://www.bizjournals.com/kansascity/news/2015/10/14/alterra-bank-co-founder-switches-gears-to-trucking.html.

9   Greenawald, Erin. 2019. "A Truly Noble Experiment: Leaving Finance To Open A Rum Distillery". *Themuse.Com*. https://www.

might expect. She started out her career in finance and was very successful, working for a hedge fund with dreams of getting into venture capital at some point. This all changed when Bridget decided to leave finance and open, The Noble Experiment, her own craft rum distillery.

In an interview conducted by a woman named Erin Greenawald, she gives us a lot of insight into her life and shares her story of this great career pivot.

She was first asked the question that you are definitely wondering, why a rum distillery, what made her switch to that?

> *"I was working for a hedge fund as part of its consumer staples team. About a year into it, I stumbled across a stock for a beer manufacturer, and ultimately kind of landed myself as a global alcoholic beverage analyst. I spent about four and a half years researching and investing in globally traded beer, wine, and spirits companies. Over time, I just developed a huge passion for the people behind handmade stuff and the research that's in craft beer and vineyards domestically and internationally.*

themuse.com/advice/a-truly-noble-experiment-leaving-finance-to-open-a-rum-distillery.

I always wanted to own my own business, but I thought it would be in finance because that's what I jumped into in school. I was evaluating my next move in finance to get myself to the place where I could open my own financial institution, and I was really hoping to get into venture capital just because new business excited me. And then I realized that I didn't want to be on the outside looking in any-more—I really wanted to get my hands dirty and own my own business.

Really, the motivation behind the idea is to incorporate the history of rum distillation in the Northeast. It was the first spirit we actually distilled in this country, and I want to help bring it back and make it as distinc-tive to this space as possible. So we're using three ingredients: New York tap water that's been filtered, molasses from sugar cane farms in Florida and Louisiana, and our propri-etary yeast strain. All the processes are done here and the aged stuff, when it's ready to be released, will be aged here."

Seeing that her early years all went to finance she was also asked how she managed to learn the skills needed to take on this new venture.

> *"I was very self-taught. I'm really naturally math and science oriented, so when I decided I was going to do this, I spent about a year studying on my own while I was writing the business plan and trying to get money. I read everything I possibly could on fermentation science and distillation science, and I continue to read as much as I can. There's a great book that's pretty technical called The Complete Distiller—it's the best resource that I've found.*
>
> *I also visited as many small distilleries as I could drive to in New York and took a trip out to Kentucky to visit the big bourbon guys there and pick their brains. Then once we were finishing construction, I spent the first two to three months doing a trial and error process to get to the final outcome.*
>
> *Education is a conundrum in the industry in general right now. Domestic distilling has been nascent since just prior to Prohibition, and it's just coming back. While the smart*

thing to do from a business standpoint would be to hire a distiller or hire someone to consult with, those people hardly exist in this country. There's no formal education—you can't get a degree in brewing and distilling. I would say 90-95% of small craft distillers these days have no background in it. They're all self-taught.

But a lot of distillers around the country are very much willing to share their methods. I happen to be very transparent about how things are done. That's not going to teach you how to do everything, but every little bit helps."

As we all know finance pays pretty well, but aside from that it was a guaranteed pay day every 2 weeks, so she was asked what it was like moving away from that stability, her answer:

"I think you hit the nail on the head—you're getting a paycheck every two weeks. You have health insurance. And I happened to be in a ridiculously cushy job where I was getting paid a lot of money as a young person.

There's nothing I can say that can explain the transition to being fully accountable for your-self and your company and then for investors.

And while it's extremely empowering—I'm in control, I have nobody to blame but myself— it's a completely double-edged sword. It's challenging in that you don't have that guaranteed payment and you don't know when you're going to have that again.

That can cause a lot of anxiety, and if you harp on that it can become paralyzing. So you just have to keep moving forward and striving to get better, and achieve your goals in a different way."

When asked what advice she would give to someone considering a major career pivot she responded:

"I would 100% encourage somebody to do this. The amount that I have learned in the past two years—writing a 30-page business plan with financials, sourcing money, figuring out how I'm going to fund something, getting the licensing required, drawing up legal documents for the business, actually working with an architect to build the space, filing with the city, managing contractors—is irreplaceable. Doing it all yourself is the most empowering feeling.

I was completely inspired to do this. That feeling was like nothing's going to stop me. If you have that feeling—if you have that passion for something—you will succeed."

PIVOT Point #12 - Use your curiosity and opportunity to be catalysts to career transitions.

It is said that we lose a lot of our curiosity when we go from childhood to adulthood. If you can manage to keep your little spark of curiosity you'd be surprised at all the amazing things that can bring. Curiosity may have killed the cat but it's also what birthed some of our greatest inventions to date. It may end up leading to an opportunity that gives you the best experience of your career, just like it did for Jeff and Bridget.

PIVOT Point #13 - Research, research, research.

Getting smart on whatever new industry you want to pivot toward is going to be one of the most important things you can do for your transition. Anyone can say that they want to change career paths, but you will not be successful if you do not know what you're getting yourself into. Research this new industry or job function.

CHAPTER 7

RISKY

———

The biggest risk is not taking any risk. ... In a world that's changing really quickly, the only strategy that is guaranteed to fail is not taking risks.

—MARK ZUCKERBERG

* * *

THE SPEECH OR THE GAME

What do I choose: the Speech or the Game? This thought kept playing over and over in my head. I was so torn, but why? Basketball was still the most important thing in the world to me right? Wasn't it?

So why isn't this an easy decision?

But it was. I gave the speech…How did I get to a place where I didn't choose basketball?

Let's rewind a couple days to get a better understanding of what's going on.

I had just gotten back from my study abroad trip in Europe and things were moving fast. It was now my sophomore year at Rockland Community College, but something was different. My mindset had completely changed—or, at least, it was in the process of completely changing. I viewed a lot of things differently at that point. It was actually interesting to see the deep internal conflict within me with this new perspective. During this time my favorite place to be became the honors office, because there I always had people to share my thoughts with and that helped me with processing everything.

So when did this conflict begin? How did it all start? Well, the conflict started right before the trip actually, but it was way different upon returning back to Rockland Community College the following semester. I had not expected it to be so hard when getting back. I began asking myself more pressing questions such as:

What's wrong?

What's so different?

Did my mindset change this much in such a short period of time?

Is it a problem of basketball not meaning as much to me anymore or something else just meaning more to me now?

At the start of this new semester I experienced a scheduling conflict, one that could not be avoided. The honors macroeconomics class I had decided to take overlapped with the men's basketball team practice time, and not just by a few minutes—it was a significant conflict. Practice was supposed to start at 3 p.m. and go until about 6 p.m., while the class started at 3 p.m. and ended at 4:15 p.m. It was not like I just blatantly wanted to miss practice, but I sort of had to: this class was only offered one time this semester, and that was the time it was offered. My coach was not very happy about this, nor did I expect him to be—he never really cared too much about us off the basketball court.

* * *

I had received an email from Hannah in the honors office stating that she, and the head of the honors program, Dr. Lynch, wanted to see me in the office as soon as possible. I did not know what was going on or what to expect. I did not know whether it was good or bad. Just in case it was time-sensitive, I decided to go right away. When I got there I was greeted by the two of them. Dr. Lynch tried right away to assure me that nothing was wrong and apologized if she had scared me. I told them "it's no big deal" and "I'm fine" but then asked what the situation was about.

"We want you to give a speech on behalf of the honors program, telling your story."

—Dr. Lynch

At that moment all I could think in my head was, *really why me? What was so special about my story.* But of course I didn't say that, I told them that I would think about it and let them know soon.

After that meeting, I continued along with the rest of my day, everything going smoothly up until I arrived late to practice due to my scheduling conflict, so I got right into it. I made sure to stretch in the locker room and warmed up a little bit so I could jump right into the drills. I noticed at the end of the drills that Coach was putting a lot of focus into the plays. He was trying to make sure that all of the newest players were understanding the plays and knew where they needed to be on the court at all times. He wanted to make sure the guys could play multiple positions and knew where each position was supposed to be during every play. Being that I was one of the senior guards and always did pretty well with remembering the plays, he had me on the floor often to demonstrate to the other players what to do.

At the end of practice coach announced we had our first away game coming up, and guess what day it falls on. Just my luck.

After learning that we had our first away game on the same day I was supposed to give the speech on behalf of the honors program, I was torn. There was absolutely no way that I could do both; they were at the exact same time—7 p.m. I do not even truly believe that the real internal conflict was between whether I gave the speech or went to the game; it was because I already knew what I wanted to do and what I was going to do, and it wasn't playing in that game. How could it be so easy for me to decide this? Basketball has been my entire life since I was seven years old. Why is it so easy for me to just choose the speech?

The one thing that allowed me to keep basketball on my mind was my teammates. I had always prided myself on being a good teammate. They were my family, my brothers. I could not let them down. Who was going to provide that senior leadership? All of our other guards were first-years and had never played college basketball before. Who was going to be there to show them the differences between high school and college? The difference in pace? In size? My teammates needed me, or at least I felt like they did. It seemed my coach didn't share the same opinion by the way he was treating me coming down to the last days of practice before the game. Not the head coach, but the assistant coach, because he ran practices most of the time. He would disrespect me during practice, and I was tired of the mistreatment. I approached the head coach about it, and he apologized, telling me he would talk to him. There was not a significant change, which lead me to believe they considered me expendable—that really helped with my decision-making. When my teammates told me that they would've left the team a long time ago if they got treated the way I did, that was my out. I no longer felt bad for leaving my teammates. I previously stayed not just for my love of the game but also my love for my teammates, but when they gave me their blessing, I felt like my decision was made.

A few days later...

The day of the speech and the game was now upon me, and even though I felt as though I had made my decision already, I walked with the suit for my speech but also my game gear. I stayed far away from the gym this day: I went to class, got something to eat, then stayed in the honors office all day until it was time to for the speech. Hanging out in the honors office became very therapeutic for me; it was that safe space that I needed. I felt so appreciated while in that office, the opposite of what I felt with the basketball team. It was time to give the speech and I was a bit nervous. It was my first speech since my eighth-grade graduation as salutatorian. I had no experience of this in high school at all, but it was okay because they just want me to tell my story and experiences. It's funny because a couple months before this, I would've been too terrified to even consider speaking. I used to be very shy before I studied abroad in Cambridge, but that trip truly helped me to grow and break out of my shell. I was a bit nervous, but also very excited to share my story. I started to give my speech, and once I heard that laugh from the crowd after I made my little sarcastic joke all the butterflies were gone.

The response after I had completed the speech was unreal. I am not referring to the basic applause that everyone expects after they finish talking. It was what happened after that. The questions that the high school eleventh and twelfth graders had for me—the curiosity that they showed toward me and my story—moved me. In addition to the questions about college in general, students came up to me after the program with their own private questions. The parents came up to me for advice and offered me their gratitude. It was amazing. I never knew I could be someone who had that much influence. It may have only been a handful of people, but to me that was a lot at the time. *Maybe I could become an influence on a much larger scale some day*, I thought.

* * *

PRIVATE EQUITY TO TECH ENTREPRENEUR

A major career change is always risky but some can appear to be more risky than others. Leaving your finance job at a private equity firm to create and run a technology based startup is probably as risky as it can get, yet this was the decision that Randy Rayess made. He even claims that some of the closest people to him told him their thoughts that reaffirmed the risks.

> *"Given the amount I could learn as an entre-*
> *preneur, and the contribution I could have*
> *when starting a new company, I decided to*
> *make the jump into the startup world...while*
> *this was considered very surprising to my*
> *colleagues and friends, and seemed very risky,*
> *it felt like the right thing to do."*

—Randy[10]

---

10   Brustein, Darrah. 2015. "9 Entrepreneurs Tell Their Stories Of
     Pivoting 180 Degrees To Start New Careers". *Entrepreneur*. https://
     www.entrepreneur.com/article/246965.

In an article written by Randy in TechCrunch he gave insight on the opportunity that he saw with his co-founder and why they decided to start VenturePact:

> *"My cofounder, Pratham Mittal, and I recognized that many businesses were struggling with their digital initiatives. Technology companies were finding it hard to hire great developers and non-tech businesses were having a lot of problems incorporating technology into their business. A key reason for this problem is that outsourcing software, managing remote and distributed engineering teams and hiring the best software developers full time or as freelancers is difficult. We started VenturePact. com to help businesses better address their tech needs."*[11]

Aside from everything there was one major factor that got Randy to completely commit to the transition. It was the "Regret Minimization" framework, he learned about this framework. It was the only thing that got Randy to ignore his doubts. It is a framework where you go over the regrets in your future life and he realized that VenturePact was something that he didn't want to regret.

11   Rayess, Randy. 2019. *Techcrunch.* https://techcrunch.com/author/randy-rayess/.

"I knew that if I was going to look back at my life in 50 years, I would regret not pursuing VenturePact, so I made the jump...the last few years have been an amazing ride and learning experience."

—Randy

PIVOT Point #14 — Listen to your Gut

No one knows you better than yourself, take the time to evaluate decisions and be honest with yourself. Ask yourself the important questions, like "what do you actually want to do?" After that then consider everything else and all the additional outside factors.

PIVOT Point #15 — A nice salary is very convincing but don't let it control you.

I'm not going to tell you that money isn't important or that it is not something that you should consider, all I'm saying is that it shouldn't be the only thing. Your happiness should be a factor when deciding whether a paycheck is worth it or not.

PIVOT Point #16 — Use the "regret minimization" framework when pondering a new move, especially if it's a risky one.

The "Regret Minimization" framework was created by Jeff Bezos, using this system you project yourself out to eighty years old, look back on your life, and then try to minimize the number of regrets. It helps you get past certain roadblocks that can confuse you in the short term.

CHAPTER 8

LIFE HAPPENS

———

* * *

"We all experience many freakish and unexpected events - you have to be open to suffering a little. The philosopher Schopenhauer talked about how out of the randomness, there is an apparent intention in the fate of an individual that can be glimpsed later on. When you are an old guy, you can look back, and maybe this rambling life has some through-line. Others can see it better sometimes. But when you glimpse it yourself, you see it more clearly than anyone."

—VIGGO MORTENSEN

* * *

TRAUMA LEADS TO A BAR

When you live through a tragic and traumatic event it's only natural that the way how you see things may change. That is exactly what happened to Jeremy Goldberg and it caused him to pivot.

Jeremy worked as a stockbroker in the financial district of New York City, better known as Wall Street, he worked there during the late '90s and early 2000s. He never really had a problem or issue with his job until September 11, 2001. He witnessed firsthand one the biggest terrorist attacks on United States soil, the attack on the Twin Towers (also known as the World Trade Center). Not only was he aware of the attack but working on Wall Street put him in very close proximity to where it all happened. His direct words on the matter were:

"... it affected me profoundly."

—Jeremy

He no longer wanted to just move money around, and because of this, at the age of 27 he left his job as a stock broker to produce a documentary about U.S craft beer. Then he decided to take it further and opened up the "Cape Ann Brewing Company" which was located in Gloucester, Massachusetts. Thirteen years later he had almost 50 employees

and a brick-and-mortar brewery and restaurant, something
that he was very proud of.

> *"We've had our ups and downs, struggles and*
> *triumphs; but in the end, I know I'm doing*
> *something now that while unconventional*
> *-- particularly for someone who at the time*
> *had no business taking on this kind of chal-*
> *lenge -- I am passionate about and allows*
> *me to look around and see evidence of a*
> *real accomplishment."*

—Jeremy[12]

* * *

LIFE CHANGING JOURNEYS [13]

Near death experiences have an affect on you where your life
flashes before your eyes, when that happens it gives you the
opportunity to reflect on everything that happened in your
life and you decide whether you are happy with that or not.

12 Brustein, Darrah. 2015. "9 Entrepreneurs Tell Their Stories Of
    Pivoting 180 Degrees To Start New Careers". *Entrepreneur.* https://
    www.entrepreneur.com/article/246965.
13 Braun, Adam. 2013. "The Five Phrases That Can Change Your Life:
    Adam Braun At Tedxcolumbiacollege". *Youtube.* https://www.
    youtube.com/watch?v=Z80E2kqVXkk.

For Adam Braun this happened to him at the very young age of 21 years old.

Adam was a student athlete at Brown University where he played basketball. Academics were always very important to him, he was very good at Math. When he was growing up he had dreams to work in finance at Wall Street and the way he was going he was on the path to it. Then something changed!

He watched a movie called Baraka, which was shot in 24 countries around the world. After that he had this phrase stuck in his head, "Get out of your comfort zone." He wanted to experience this feeling of uncomfortable, that's when he decided that he would participate in this program called Semester at Sea. It is a program that takes students around the world to explore developing countries. He decided he would do so without telling anyone besides his parents. He withdrew from school and quit the basketball team.

His ship left from Vancouver and his voyage started. While crossing the Pacific in the middle of winter something traumatizing happened. In January in 2005 a 60 foot rogue wave hit his boat while they were at least 900 miles from land causing the boat to lose all power and almost tip over. Adam recalls this feeling as:

"There is this feeling of certain death."

—Adam

He remembers realizing that he had to have a purpose for being alive, leaving with that mindset opened his eyes. He next remembers backpacking and while he was in India where poverty was at the lowest that he had ever witnessed, he had another eye-opening moment when talking to a child.

He asked the boy, "If you could have anything in the world right now what would it be?"

The boy answered, "A pencil."

This was so powerful to Adam he realized that there were millions of children that didn't have access to education and he decided that was his mission, to eradicate this global injustice.

At 23 when he had graduated when he was getting ready to start his career on Wall Street he got this new phrase in his head:

> *"Challenge your assumptions so that you can find your truths."*

This caused him to backpack in South America for 4 months before he started his career. He met a man while he was there who asked him for help with English so that he could teach his children. Adam thought that this was amazing and at this point knew he was going to start some sort of program to help get rid of the education injustices.

He then decided to start his career at a place where he felt would prepare him for his mission, so he became a management consultant at Bain and Company. After some time he felt like he was losing his passion. By this point he was almost 25 and he had a new phrase in his head:

"Speak the language of the person you seek to become."

While keeping his job he decided he would start a school on the side. With $25 dollars he opened a business account that would be the beginning of a program that you may have heard of before, Pencils of Promise, a non-profit that builds schools and creates programs to combat global education injustice.

* * *

DAVID DOBRIK, JASON NASH, AND THE VLOG SQUAD

For the Vlog Squad their life changing moment seemed more like career ending rather than life threatening. They are a group of young adults in their early twenties (besides Jason who is a bit older) who video blog or vlog their lives and then post them on Youtube for their millions of subscribers to view. The Vlog Squad is doing pretty well right now winning awards like the best "YouTube Ensemble" at the Annual Shorty Awards, but there was a time before the Vlog Squad was on YouTube. [14]

Before the squad got together most of them got their start on a platform called Vine. Vine was a video hosting service where its user would share 6 second videos. Twitter owned Vine and decided to pull the plug on it. When that happened a lot of famous Viners panicked but then pivoted over to YouTube.[15]

David Dobrik is basically the leader of the Vlog Squad. He didn't always have the most followers but now it safe to say that he is the most popular out of the group with over 12 million subscribers on YouTube. He has won many awards

14 "Vlog Squad - The Shorty Awards". 2019. *Shortyawards.Com.* https://shortyawards.com/10th/vlog-squad.

15 Fiegerman, Seth. 2017. "Twitter Officially Shuts Down Vine". *Cnnmoney.* https://money.cnn.com/2017/01/17/technology/vine-shuts-down/index.html.

for his work. When he started on Vine he still lived with his parents back in Chicago but then decided to pack it all up and move to Los Angeles. When Vine died he started his Vlog that has become very popular.

Jason Nash who is David's main partner in crime has a very different story than the rest of the members. He is the oldest at 46 years old, double the age of David. Nash's story is interesting because he went through the more traditional forms of media first, for example television. He developed shows for major media outlets like NBC, Fox, and Oxygen. After that, he switched over to Vine where he quickly gained popularity. When Vine shut down he performed stand up comedy until he was approached by David at one of his shows. He jumped at the opportunity to do YouTube and loved the fact that you go straight to the audience with this platform, he no longer had to get his sketches approved. He now has over 2 million subscribers and loves what he does.[16]

16   Freeman, Abigail. 2019. "For Jason Nash, Life Is One Long You-tube Video". https://www.bostonglobe.com/business/2019/01/21/jason-nash-has-turned-fun-into-profession/FbCmhzKc-C23QQK6gpppPRM/story.html.

PIVOT Point #17 — Life-changing moments are signs and you should pay attention to them.

Monumental or life-changing are called those names for a reason, they may affect the way how feel or the way how we view things, it is important to not ignore these moments.

PIVOT Point #18 — Stay aware of changing times as they often bring new opportunities.

We live in a time where the world is moving so fast and constantly changing if you pay attention and are adaptable you can take full advantage of new opportunities that present themselves.

OPINIONS

CHAPTER 9

BUILD YOUR BOARD OF DIRECTORS

———

A mentor is someone who allows you to see the hope inside yourself.

—OPRAH WINFREY

* * *

MY FIRST REAL MENTOR

"I actually retired at forty years old, I just teach now because I enjoy it and travel in the summer," said the teacher of my "Principles of Finance" class, better known as Professor Repic.

This was one of the classes for my new major, once I switched from engineering to business administration. I was now very interested in what he had to say. I had so many questions that I could not ask all at once especially during class. What did he do before this? How old is he? Where is he from? How much money is enough to retire? Is what he did still possible? Why is he so passionate about teaching that he does it even though he doesn't need to?

I had so many questions, he was so interesting, he seemed so sure of himself about everything. I was so intrigued that I started staying after class to ask questions, going to his office hours, and even joining the entrepreneurship club that he was the faculty advisor for. He never sent me away, he never was too busy for me, he would answer all of my questions and challenge me to think deeper.

He opened up my mind to the inner workings of the business world. I had so many questions that couldn't be answered at home, not because my mom didn't care but because she didn't know herself. Having him as a mentor throughout my community college years and even now has been unbelievably amazing.

Professor George Repic is also single handedly responsible for me opening my first investment accounts, my first retirement account, and my first credit card account.

I will forever be grateful to professor Repic because if he did not start me down this path, it is likely that my Pivot may have never happened. To this day he is still someone who reaches out on every major holiday.

* * *

THE GEORGETOWN VISIT

It was during my first semester of my last year at Rockland Community College when I decided that I would be taking a trip to visit Georgetown University. The decision came after talking to a few of my mentors. We had come to the conclusion that I should visit as many of the schools that I was interested in as possible, and all of the schools I had down were great choices, but the real question was whether I would be a good fit.

I emailed the dean of the business school, per the advice of one of my mentors, and asked for a meeting in person sometime that week. She replied that Thursday morning would work best for her. Thursday was two days away, so I decided that I would drive down to Washington, D.C., after class Wednesday evening. It was not one of my best decisions with how tired I was, but I would definitely make the same decision if placed in the same situation again. Luckily I have an aunt who lives in D.C., and she's always willing to make space for me. Most of the ride was filled with traffic, until I crossed the Delaware Memorial Bridge when I saw clear road. My eyes lit up and my right foot got heavier on the gas—then my happy thoughts were gone when I saw the blue and red lights flashing behind me.

I pulled over to the side of the street to realize that this was a construction zone and that fines were doubled in this area. My mom was not going to be happy about this, but there was nothing I could do about it now.

When the officer approached the car he asked, "Do you know how fast you were going?"

"No sir, I'm actually not sure."

"You were going about 70 mph in a construction zone, where you're not supposed to be going over 40 mph."

"Oh wow, I'm really sorry!"

"Do you have your license and registration?"

"Yes sir," I said as I handed over the documents.

"Hmm, New York—what are you doing all the way out here?"

"Well, I'm actually on my way to D.C. for a school visit at Georgetown University."

"What are you planning on studying?"

"I'm currently double majoring in liberal arts and business administration at Rockland Community College, but I'm planning on hopefully transferring into the business school to double major in management and probably finance."

"Wow, that's amazing. Hold on; I'll be right back," the officer said as he left with my documents.

A few minutes later he approached the vehicle with a piece of paper in his hands as well as my original documents.

"This is just a warning: be safe on the rest of the drive to D.C., follow the speed limit, and good luck with school."

"Thank you so much, have a great night!" I said with the biggest smile on my face. I was so happy to not incur that expense that I could not hide the smile. I took this as a small sign that I may be making the right move visiting Georgetown, pivoting down this path may be exactly what I need to do.

I drove the rest of the way to my aunt's house without any issues and greeted her, then hopped right into bed. I had a big day ahead of me and needed to be ready for it.

The next morning, I woke up so ready to go. My aunt had ironed my clothes and prepared an amazing breakfast for me. I proceeded to get ready and then leave a bit early just to ensure that I got there on time—after all, first impressions do mean a lot.

ARRIVING AT GEORGETOWN

I arrived with time to spare, so when I parked the car I slowly walked around campus trying to find the business school. It was my first time at Georgetown's campus, so I had no idea where it was; I began asking random strangers for directions. In no time I found it. There it was: the McDonough School of Business. I had seen many pictures online after doing tons of research, but still, seeing it in person was just a breathtaking experience. I walked into this enormous building and was once again lost, but instead of searching, this time I immediately asked for help. I was directed to the dean's office not too far from the entrance of the school. When I walked in the office, I was greeted by student worker, who asked if I had an appointment. I replied "yes, with Dean Grant," and she had me take a seat while she checked me in. Dean Grant then walked out front to greet me and then took me to her office for us to talk. It was a great talk; I shared my story with her and listened to her story as well. She notified me that she had a meeting in a few minutes but wanted me to meet a student, so she asked if I could come back in a couple hours. "Of course," I said. She asked if I had gone on a tour—I told her no but I would love to. She then had the student worker whom I'd met in the front give me a tour of the business school.

After the tour I had a couple hours to kill before going back to meet with Dean Grant again, and being that I hadn't formally toured the school yet, I decided to take advantage of Georgetown's tour groups. They had tours running very regularly so I thought it would be a good idea. It was. This school was beautiful in my eyes. It was not very big, but it did remind me of Cambridge a little bit. The architecture was completely different, but I could see and feel the history while walking through campus something that I also remember feeling when roaming Cambridge's campus. I was the only transfer in the group of the tour, and I think everyone could probably tell, seeing as I was the only person there without a parent with me, yet it was still a great tour.

MEETING A STUDENT MENTOR

The time had passed and it was time to go back to Dean Grant's office. I was very excited to meet the student that

Dean Grant thought I should know. I walked into the dean's office and was greeted by a pleasant smile and a handshake from the student. He asked if my name was Derron, then he introduced himself as Febin. We talked for a bit then walked back to Dean Grant's office. She was happy to see that we had met and introduced ourselves already. She had notified him that I was planning on transferring into Georgetown's business school from Rockland Community College, the same way he did. He asked me if I had sat in on a class and I said no. Then Dean Grant asked if I would be in the area still tomorrow, and when I replied yes she immediately emailed the professor and got a response. I was going to sit in on a three-hour business law class. I was excited and thanked her for the opportunity.

Febin and I then left the business school and he showed me around Georgetown for a bit, on that walk I realized that he was one of the most passionate people I have ever met. Since coming to he managed to start a program called "Unsung Heroes" that got a lot of national attention. It was a social venture recognizing the unsung heroes around campus. He told me that he wanted to continue this project full time after he graduated, this was not something that people in business at Georgetown typically did. He was one of the first people to not only tell me but also show me that I didn't need to follow the status quo. I had a passion for social entrepreneurship as well, and Febin ended becoming not only a friend but also a mentor to me. He still someone that I reach out to for advice from time to time.

PIVOT Point #19 — Find yourself some mentors.

Align yourself with people who are in places or positions that you want to be in, show genuine curiosity and interest. In the end the mentor has to decide whether they will guide you or not, but continuously surrounding yourself with these types of people increases your chances. Ask a lot of questions and be a sponge, soak up as much information as possible.

PIVOT Point #20 — Pay it forward.

Never forget about all of the people who mentored you before, if you are in a position to do the same then pay it forward. Aside from it being the right thing to do, it will also greatly increase your future network with powerful people willing to help you.

CHAPTER 10

SUPPORT SYSTEM PART 1 - FRIENDS, FAMILY

_____

There is no such thing as a self-made man. We are made up of thousands of others. Everyone who has ever done a kind deed for us, or spoken one word of encouragement to us, has entered into the make-up of our character and of our thoughts, as well as our success.

—GEORGE BURTON ADAMS

* * *

The support of family and friends can truly affect how we proceed with certain decisions in life. We all want the approval and support of our loved ones, they are the closest people in our lives so it only makes sense.

MY BROTHER'S KEEPER

Upon my return from studying abroad at the University of Cambridge, my mindset had truly changed, and my older cousin, Alan, had definitely noticed. I was at his house on a Saturday night, as I was most weekends. We were in his room just talking about life and then Cambridge came up. I was speaking so passionately about it and was very adamant in stating that it was the best experience of my life—at that point, he realized the trip was truly transformative for me. He then explained to me he had never been to Europe before but that it was one of his life goals to go. I told him the experience was second to none and that he should definitely get out there when he gets a chance. He asked me if I would go out to Europe again and I told him that I would do it in a heartbeat. My cousin's childhood was a lot different than mine. He was born in Trinidad and Tobago, the same country my parents are from, and he lived his early childhood years there. He moved up to the United States at a pretty young age, but he was not a citizen so he did not receive all the same benefits that an American child would receive or have the chance to chase the same opportunities. At this point in his life when we were having the conversation, he had recently gotten his citizenship and was in the process of searching for a new job.

My cousin did end up getting a new job, and not just a regular job—a unionized one that would pay him pretty well and give him great benefits. Alan was more like a brother to me than a cousin so it was an extremely proud and happy moment for me when he told me that he had gotten this new job. He really deserved it, or at least I felt like he did. It was perfect for him, and not a very long commute at all, so it seemed like his dreams would be able to start becoming realities now. And they did. He was able to buy his dream bike: a Harley Davidson.

SPONTANEOUS FLIGHTS

My phone began to ring on a random Sunday night in January and I looked at the caller ID and it read "Alan." This was not strange, though, because we called and talked to each other all the time, so I picked up the phone.

"Remember when you said you would go back to Europe in a heartbeat? Well, do you want to go this summer?" he asked as soon as heard me pick up.

"Wait what?" I responded, sort of confused.

"I see two roundtrip tickets to England right now for a little under seven hundred dollars each. If you are serious about going and can save up at least a thousand dollars, I'll buy the tickets right now. You have to decide now though; these are the last two tickets at this price," he said with slight anxiety in his voice almost as though to let me know that this was time-sensitive.

"Yes you can 100 percent count me in," I responded with confidence—I was working twenty hours a week in addition to school so I knew I should be able to afford it.

"Okay, cool. I'll let you know when I figure out the rest of the details," he said as he was getting ready to hang up.

"Sounds like a plan," I answered and then concluded the call.

THE TRUST

A couple weeks later, Alan called me offering me a great opportunity. He was willing to co-sign for me to get a charge card under him. Did he really have that much trust in me? Was I really getting such a great opportunity placed in front of me like this? What did I do to deserve this? Was this what it is like having an older brother? Yes, this is exactly what it is like, having someone who has come before you and who cares about you, making your path easier. This card came with so many benefits—especially travel benefits—but it also came with many rules, which makes sense for a card of its magnitude. Alan let me know that his credit would be affected by anything stupid that I decided to do but that he was confident in how responsible that I was and trusted me not to ruin his credit.

PLANNING

I received another phone call from Alan, and at this point, it seemed like we were ready to start planning our Euro trip. He asked me if I had a preference between Prague or Paris and I responded no, because I had not been tThe Art of the Pivoto either, so I would be cool with going to either of those places. I told him I am actually very indecisive and that it would take me pretty long to make most of the decisions on where we should go. I let him know again that I have only been to Europe once before and it was to England, so I'm interested in going just about anywhere. He decided we would go from England, to Prague in the Czech Republic, then to Munich in Germany, then back to the United Kingdom before we would fly home. I let him know of my approval for the trip and he started working out the logistics with flights and where we would stay. Then he let me know that with the charge card I get a free priority pass, which gives you access to the lounges in airports, and free global entry, which lets you skip the ridiculously long but necessary customs lines. He told I had to sign up for these things, so I agreed and made a plan to get them done.

THE TRIP OF A LIFETIME

It was now the end of July—time for my Euro trip with Alan. Because it was an international flight, we had to get there relatively early and so we do. However, with the global entry pass it didn't take us very long to get through security, so we had a lot of time before our flight to just relax and check out the lounge we had free access to. It was actually amazing walking into the lounge for the first time: you are treated with so much care and everything there is so comfortable it almost makes you want to just stay there and not go to your flight. That's probably why each lounge has an hour limit of how long you can stay. These lounges offered free food and drinks, as well as comfortable seats, and some lounges even offer massages. I had such a great time in the lounge that I decided from now on whenever I went to the airport no matter how short the time was I would make an appearance at the lounge.

THE ENGLISH EXPERIENCE

Landing in England for the second time in my life was just as exciting as landing in England for the first time. I tried to get as much sleep as I could on the plane even though it was very difficult, especially because of how cramped it was in there. I knew with the time difference I should try to get as much sleep as possible to try to avoid the jet lag but it couldn't be avoided. Not that it mattered much though, because with all the adrenaline pumping through me I found it very difficult to catch any shut-eye once I stepped off that plane. England was amazing; I loved being immersed in this culture, and I got to see many different extraordinary things while I was here, such as Stonehenge, for example. Alan also had a friend living in England who took us to his hometown where we got to go to Top Golf. It was my first time there, even though they have if you locations in the States. It was one of the most fun places to hang out at that I had ever been to.

THE BEAUTY OF PRAGUE

Getting the opportunity to go to Prague was very special, especially at the time we were there. There was a social media post going around the Internet then of a celebrity bragging about taking a private jet to Prague. So being able to experience this place at the same time made it even more amazing. I was even able to make my own version of the video that I only shared with family and friends. Stepping off the plane and into Prague was a much different feeling than arriving in England: this was literally the first time I was in a country where the primary language was not English. It was such a unique experience for me at first, looking at all of the signs and trying to figure out what they meant. It became almost like a little fun game to me. Leaving the airport and actually getting into the city, I realized how pretty it was. It was the prettiest place I had ever seen in my life (not that I had lived that long anyway but still just breathtaking). I loved witnessing all the castles and the extraordinary architecture of the buildings.

BIKES IN GERMANY

Getting to Germany was very cool, especially because here we got to experience their train system, which was pretty simple to figure out how to use. During our entire trip, Munich was the shortest stop, which is my only regret from the entire backpacking experience. Getting there I realized that Munich had some of the best food and also some of the most fun places to visit. There was a river that I got to experience while there that was essentially just like a beach. People would line up on both sides of the river and lay out sunbathing or actually swimming and having a great time in the water. I was surprised to see the amount of people that would go to the river; I'm not exactly sure how long the river was but there were people packed on both sides for as long as I could see. We also decided to rent bikes while in Munich as they had a very advanced bike lane system that we wanted to try out, and it was so much fun, way better than riding bikes back home.

BOATS IN AMSTERDAM

Amsterdam was a place of many mysteries until I got there and saw it for myself. It looked just as it looked on the television and computer screen. I had never experienced anything else like it, walking down streets that were right next to canals. Being able to drive and then look right next to you and see a boat down in the canal. I rented a bike while here in Amsterdam as well and it was a very fun time—a little more dangerous than in Germany but still worth it. One thing that I did get to do in Amsterdam that I couldn't do anywhere else was drive a boat through the canals. It was a little nerve-wracking when getting out into the open water with much bigger boats, but worth it all the same.

EXPERIENCING THE CLIFFS IN BEACHY HEAD

Flying back into England, I didn't expect it to be so moving the second time around as well. This time we went to a much different place, called Beachy Head. It was the most beautiful place in England, I thought; I had not seen the entirety of England, of course, but Beachy Head was so beautiful I could almost guarantee no other place in England could top it. Alan loves bikes and had a friend up in Beachy Head who was going to take him riding. I did not know how to ride motorbikes at the time—and I still don't—so I rode behind them in a van. There were some cliffs we stopped to see, one of the most amazing sites to see in the world, a place so movie-worthy. Hearing the history behind the area and how it was actually a very popular spot for suicide sort of made me look at it a little differently, but it was still a place I think everyone should see one day.

REFLECTION

Finally, while sitting in the airport getting ready to leave to come back to New York I got the opportunity to reflect on the trip I just had. It opened my eyes to a lot of different things, let me know that there was so much more out there, gave me so much more perspective. I wanted other kids from neighborhoods like mine to be able to get the same experiences, as none of my other close friends had gotten an experience like this. I wanted there to be more exposure and awareness of things like this in my community, as well as other minority communities. Then I thought, *Why can't I be the one to start this campaign?* I had already realized I loved entrepreneurship, and I could use this as the avenue to empower our youth. This entire experience came out of a conversation I had with my older cousin—I'm sure he didn't know what the exact impact would be, but he thought this trip would be beneficial for me and he couldn't have been more right.

* * *

FROM LAW TO CUPCAKES[17]

Often, it is not our own fears of stepping out of our comfort zone or deviating from our original career paths, but our lingering fears that we will be a disappointment to someone else that hold us back.

For a woman named Lisa Song Sutton this was the exact case when she wanted to veer into a new career. She had a great job with a nice salary, good benefits, and giving all of that up is not what bothered her, it was the thought of potentially unhappy parents. Lisa worked as an associate and VP of Human Resources at a law firm. She didn't believe that her parents, who put her through her undergraduate years at the University of Arizona and through her graduate school years at the University of Miami, would like her throwing away prestigious career. Despite these feelings she decided to start her own alcohol-infused cupcake company.[18]

"When I transitioned from working as an associate and VP of human resources in a law firm to founding an alcohol-infused cupcake company, the hardest part wasn't walking

---

17 Brustein, Darrah. 2015. "9 Entrepreneurs Tell Their Stories Of Pivoting 180 Degrees To Start New Careers". *Entrepreneur.* https://www.entrepreneur.com/article/246965.

18 Siu, Eric. 2019. "How Miss Nevada Lisa Song Built A $2M/Year Alcohol-Infused Cupcake Empire". Podcast. *Growth Everywhere Podcast.*

away from the salary, the steady job, or the
perceived prestige of my occupation; the most
difficult part was telling my parents!"

—Lisa

To her surprise her parents were just happy that she was following her own dreams, they were proud of her for wanting to be her own boss. With all of the success that she has had with Sin City Cupcakes, I believe that both her and her parents know that she made the right decision.

PIVOT Point #21 — Embrace those who embrace you.

Accept genuine support from wherever it comes from, for me it was from my older cousin who has become a big brother to me. He has become such an influential person in my life and I truly appreciate that. He is also that person that I can talk to about anything, and having someone like this is very important especially with all of the stress that can come from a veer in your career path.

PIVOT Point #22 — Don't be afraid to disappoint your family and friends.

For our own happiness we will sometimes have to make decisions that everyone will not approve of but if these people are true friends and family they will support you anyway, and will be glad to see you happy.

CHAPTER 11

SUPPORT SYSTEM PART 2 - THE MICHELLE TO MY BARACK

———

"Obviously I couldn't have done anything that I've done without Michelle...not only has she been a great first lady, she is just my rock. I count on her in so many ways every single day."

—PRESIDENT BARACK OBAMA

* * *

The choice of our significant other serves as one of the most important decisions that we will ever make, especially when it comes to the case of your pivot. They will have the power to make your metamorphosis easier or harder. It takes the support of your significant other to facilitate a smooth transition.

You and your significant other are partners; in life, love, finances and beyond. When you consider your Pivot of choice, you must also consider the sacrifices that your significant other will perform on your behalf. Be honest with your partner and make sure you find a way to offer a compromise that will benefit your partner as well. The last thing you want is for your Pivot to ruin your relationship.

FROM STABLE DATA ANALYSIS TO FREELANCE WRITING[19]

"When I was a child, dreaming about being a veterinarian, I believed that my career would be determined by my passions . I thought that whatever made me the happiest would be the way I spent my days.

By the time I got to high school, I was considering business management or marketing—I thought that a substantial paycheck would

---

19 Cross, Lindsay. 2019. "Why I Left A Steady Gig To Be A Freelance Writer". *Themuse.Com.* https://www.themuse.com/advice/why-i-left-a-steady-gig-to-be-a-freelance-writer.

be the most influential factor in my occupa-
tional pursuits."

—Lindsay Cross

Like most people Lindsay changed her mind a few times about what she wanted to do for a career. But to be fair how many high school students truly know what they want to do for the rest of their professional lives.

Lindsay started her career after college working in data analysis at a midsized alcohol distribution company. It was a very stable job with stable hours . According to Cross "the job came with paid vacation time, healthcare benefits, and a generous retirement package." In other words, it seemed like a very comfortable place to work for many adults, and on top of that, this is where she met her husband. Not to mention she was also very good at the job so she got promoted faster than normal and was awarded more responsibility. You could imagine that this would be a perfect scenario and for Lindsay looking from the outside in it was.

In her free time Lindsay would read articles from this fashion website, and on one bit of her downtime at work she decided to email the editor of one of the articles. This ended up becoming an opportunity to write a piece about stylish motherhood, which turned into an opportunity for her to write one piece a week which became a hobby for her.

Then the company ended up launching a parenting website and she started writing everyday. She spent lunch hours as well as her nights writing stories. Her husband was very supportive and took on a lot of the responsibility in the house.

> *"At home, the minute that dinner was done,*
> *my husband took over with our daughter, and*
> *I sat down to type."*

> —Lindsay

What started as a pastime passion started to become difficult because of having to focus on her day job.

> *"...after four months of trying to juggle what*
> *had become two full-time jobs, I decided*
> *that I had to make a choice. Life couldn't go*
> *on like this."*

> —Lindsay

She had a tough decision to make, does she stay with her comfortable data analysis job or does she go with her passion, writing?

There was so much for her to consider, she had a family, she was a wife as well as a mother. She had to figure out taxes, retirement, salary changes, job benefits, healthcare coverage, probably too much for any one person to figure out on their own. So with that in mind she decided to go research and get the knowledge to have a well informed discussion with her husband.

They first discussed the stuff that they could quantify, things like the difference in pay. Lindsay realized that her and their daughter would qualify for healthcare coverage under her husbands plan but the price would go up.

After getting past all of the quantifiable stuff, they decided to discuss the things that you couldn't measure with a number, like personal happiness. Her husband's main concern was which job gave her the most satisfaction, he had a consistent full-time job which gave them the financial stability to take a pay cut.

> *"...he was supportive of whatever decision I made. That said, freelancing provided the type of flexibility that many working parents dream of—I would be able to volunteer in my daughter's classroom, and still work when she was home sick."*

Lindsay final decision was to continue freelance writing but with all things considered this was definitely not something she could not do with the help and support of her husband.

AMAZON'S BIRTH

Back in Chapter 7 we talked about the "Regret Minimization" framework that Jeff created and while that was a big reason he decided to make his career change, we didn't talk about the huge role his wife played in the matter.

Bezos worked at a New York City hedge fund, D.E. Shaw. When he first came up with the idea for an online bookstore he told his boss, this led to a 2 hour walk through Central Park in New York City. The conclusion of their conversation:

"This actually sounds like a really good idea to me but it sounds like it would be an even better idea for someone who didn't already have a good job."[20]

It was a different conversation when he told his wife MacKenzie, she was very supportive and excited for him, something that I believed definitely helped influence his decision.

---

20   Bezos, Jeff. 2008. "Jeff Bezos - Regret Minimization Framework". *Youtube.* https://www.youtube.com/watch?v=jwG_qR6XmDQ.

"And to me, you know, watching your spouse, somebody that you love, have an adventure — what is better than that, and being part of that?"

—MacKenzie (in a CBS interview)[21]

But not only did she just give positive words of affirmation, she showed her support through her actions. In 1994, they took a road trip from New York City to Seattle, on that trip she helped Jeff create Amazon's business plan. She also became the company's first accountant and helped negotiated Amazon's first freight contracts.

It was MacKenzie's help that facilitated Jeff's pivot.

PIVOT Point #23 - Choose your relationships wisely and consider the sacrifices that your partner will endure on your behalf

Your choice of a significant other provided you decide to have one, will prove to be one of the most important decisions you

---

21 Abadi, Mark. 2019. "Mackenzie Bezos Played A Big Role In The Founding Of Amazon And Drove Across The Country With Jeff To Start It". *Business Insider*. https://www.businessinsider.com/ how-mackenzie-bezos-met-jeff-bezos-2019-1.

will ever make. The decisions that either of you make will no longer just affect one person. Finding someone who accepts you for who you are is important. It is also important to find someone who is open minded enough to accept you for who you are. But most importantly you have to find someone who is supportive.

When someone decides to pivot or make a big life change there's a lot of baggage that comes with that, and unless you are alone this will affect your significant other. It is important to remember to stay honest and consider all that they will have to endure as well. Having a conversation with them before any final decisions are made would be ideal.

* * *

TRANSITION

CHAPTER 12

NOT LOOKING BACK

———

If you're walking down the right path and you're willing to keep walking, eventually you'll make progress.

—PRESIDENT BARACK OBAMA

* * *

When a pivot happens, it can be a difficult process to adjust, but it's important to continue to push forward if you feel like it was the right transition for you.

It was only a couple months into my first semester at Georgetown University, which had so many ups and downs, but most people couldn't tell unless I absolutely wanted them to.

I usually strolled around with a smile planted on my face hoping to brighten up someone else's day.

I was going through my first midterm season, and things were not going as seamlessly as I thought they were—but hey, this is Georgetown, right? I had to have known that the work here would be harder than that of my community college. Plus there are so many opportunities there that the good outweighed the bad anyway. I could adjust to the difficult and intensive workload, but I couldn't get these opportunities just anywhere.

I would go to every event possible at first in the business school when I got into Georgetown. I was really trying to find my fit and specifically meet some new people hopefully who had similar likes or interests as me. There was this one networking event where underclassmen got to meet seniors who'd had a successful internship the summer before, and most likely had return offers to work full time upon graduation. I talked to a few different people at this event, but there was one person who I was very interested in connecting with. In the business school there are not very many people of my race in my classes, and at this event there was one. That's specifically why I wanted to connect with this one person: I wanted to ask her about different diversity programs or things that she did to help her succeed. She shared a lot of information with me and told me she wanted to introduce me to someone via email. So she gave me her email and I emailed her after the event and then she sent an email connecting me to a student named Jerome Smalls, a junior in the business school.

Jerome then sent me an email and we worked out a time for us to meet up to talk in person. We decided that we would meet in Lau, the campus's main library. Upon this first meeting with him, we shared a lot of different information about ourselves to each other and I felt as though I learned a lot. We had a lot of similarities—not as in things like where we're from, but more so stuff we are both passionate about such as mentoring the youth and entrepreneurship. I told him about an idea that I had for a startup, and then he told me an idea that he had for a startup. I was actually blown away that we got along so well at first. It was actually great finding someone who had similar interests; this made for an easy person to talk to, as well as making it easier to explain things because I felt like there was this pre-understanding.

I decided that I was going to go all in with my startup idea and try to utilize all the resources at Georgetown. So I looked on the Startup Hoyas' website and scrolled through the different resources and found the entrepreneurs in residence. I learned that we had a few different entrepreneurs in residence who were all experts in their own respective fields or sectors. I found someone whose expertise was in social ventures and startups, so I decided to sign up for office hours—one of the best decisions I've ever made. After meeting with her only one time, I formulated a much more concise plan as to what I was going to do with my startup. Like which direction I wanted it to go in. Not only was she very smart and super knowledgeable in this area and space, but she was also very supportive and encouraging.

I decided to meet with Fiona again, the expert entrepreneur in residence. Now my plan made a lot more sense, was a bit more concise, and had a valid direction to go in. After hearing these new advancements, she told me that I should enter the Startup Hoyas Rocket Pitch Competition. I literally did not know what to say: I had never pitched in a pitch competition before, but this seemed like a great opportunity. It was not something that I had to think long and hard about. I told her within a couple minutes that I would definitely do it if she thought that I was ready. She let me know that the rocket pitch competition would only be two-minute pitches, and no slides. This meant that I only had to work on perfecting a two-minute pitch, something that I thought was very doable.

Later on the same day after seeing the entrepreneur in residence, I saw Jerome in the dining hall. We had both just come from completing work so we were both relatively tired. I let him know about my encounter with Fiona and that I was going to pitch in the rocket pitch competition. After discussing it with him for a while he told me that he may end up pitching in the competition as well, and I thought this would be a great experience for the both of us with our respective startups.

* * *

CO-FOUNDING A VENTURE

After thinking it over for a long time, I started pondering the idea of Jerome and I putting our ideas together and pitching together in the rocket pitch competition. I had no idea whether he'd be for it or not, but there was only one way to find out, and that was to ask him straight up. So that's what I did, I sent a long, thought-out message to him asking if he would like to put our ideas together, be co-founders, and pitch together in the rocket pitch competition. He ended up responding saying that he would love to and that it would be better if we were co-founders so we can keep each other accountable. This was the beginning of something big.

After Jerome and I decided to partner up, we had a meeting, in which we decided that we would keep the name he'd created for his start up because it was very catchy: SmallTalk. After this new advancement, I was very excited to share the news with Fiona, as she was the entrepreneur in residence that I was meeting with through every other advancement of my entrepreneurial career so far at Georgetown. She was very happy and excited for our new direction and us coming together; she said this was the progress that she liked to see. So now it was time to work on our pitch and she was going to help us, letting us know that there was another team or group of entrepreneurs that she was helping as well. She had us all meet and then had a coaching session together with both teams present. They had a four-person team versus our two-person team. At first wary to practice with another team that was going to be our competition, I realized after the session how beneficial it was to hear their input and opinions on our pitches and how we could improve them, and vice versa.

The emails had come out for the final list of who was going to actually be presenting at the competition. Everything was fine—except for the fact that SmallTalk didn't receive an email. Being the persistent entrepreneurs that we are, we decided to email the coordinators of the pitch competition. When they got back to us, they let us know that SmallTalk actually was a finalist in the pitch competition and they apologized that we had not received an email because we were supposed to.

After hearing all of this, and after going through the coaching session with our entrepreneur in residence, and our sibling entrepreneurship team, we decided that we should practice more if we wanted to have a legitimate shot at winning. So that's exactly what we did, except both Jerome and I had really busy schedules so we couldn't find another time to meet until the night before the pitch competition. We planned on only practicing for about an hour, but we got so into it that we did not end up parting ways that night until 3 a.m. We worked on our sound, our actions, our gestures, and just us being synchronized.

PITCH DAY

The day of the pitch I had an 8 a.m. class, so I woke up after only about four hours of sleep. Then I proceeded to go through my long day of classes. Throughout the entire day I could not focus on any one class; all I could think about was the pitch competition that I would be competing in a few hours later. Jerome and I met again a couple hours before the pitch competition started, to practice some more. Then we walked together to the business school and ran through our pitches a couple more times right outside of it. Going inside, we had to sign in, and we saw how many other teams were there, a total of about twenty-five pitching that night. There were three awards—first place, second place, and the people's choice award. As the night started, it was an amazing feeling seeing such an entrepreneurial spirit in the room. Everyone was so passionate about what they were doing and what they were pitching. It also felt good to see that most of these projects had some sort of a social mission behind it. We pitched coming down to the end of the competition. There's a lot to be said pitching so late: you have seen all of the great pitches before you and it could be nerve-wracking, and you can use that to your benefit by watching the body language of the judges to see what worked on them.

After the competition ended, everyone was free to get whatever refreshments or food they wanted while we waited on the judges to present the winners. At the end of the last pitch the judges let everyone know that the poll for the people's choice award was open and that it would be displayed live. This was a very calm and peaceful moment for everyone that pitched, because you got to enjoy food while you laughed and talked with the other entrepreneurs. This was, on the other hand, a very stressful time for the judges, who had to choose between so many great ideas carried by such passionate entrepreneurs. One of my friends came up and told me that he thought we had won the people's choice award, so Jerome and I looked up the screen and saw we were in the lead. It seemed we had just won the people's choice award, and I did not know how to feel about it.

After formally getting recognized for winning the award, Jerome and I were approached by the keynote speaker of the night, the GM of mid-Atlantic Lyft, who congratulated us on our presentation and for winning the people's choice award. Our entrepreneur in residence was at the pitch competition to support us and noticed our conversation with the executive from Lyft. She approached us as he walked away and basically told us this is how you get funding and sponsorship. We then approached the executive from Lyft and talked about a possible partnership or sponsorship with Lyft, and he was very receptive and left us his email for us to contact him later. When we did, we were able to secure free transportation to and from the destinations for SmallTalk. Securing this corporate sponsorship felt similar to winning a basketball game or maybe even better.

These achievements let me know that I was on the right path: this pivot was the right one for me, and I was doing exactly what I was supposed to be doing.

PIVOT Point #24 — Take positive lessons from what you did before and apply it to your pivot.

Just because you're changing careers or transitioning to something new does not mean the lessons you learned at your previous job are obsolete; remember them and see if you can apply it on your new path. For me, I took leadership skills, competitive nature, and the ability to work well in teams, and I applied that to the things that I am now doing in the business world and I am much better off for it.

PIVOT Point #25 — Reevaluate your pivot after your transition has started and make sure it was right for you.

It is always important after any big change to reevaluate the situation and see how things are working out for you. Was it a successful pivot or not? And if not what changes could be made to ensure future success.

LETTER TO BASKETBALL

Dear Basketball,

They say when you truly love something or someone that love never completely goes away. Basketball, you will always be my first love.

I may have pivoted but I'm thankful for everything you gave me. You saved me from trouble more times than I can count. You might be the reason that I am still here today. I turned to you when the pressures of the world was just too much. You were one of the most consistent things in my life. You gave me peace, served as my safe haven, my sanctuary, my escape.

I dedicated countless hours to you, early mornings and late nights. I knew you wouldn't just hand everything to me, so I

wanted to earn it. You made me the man I am today, you made
me disciplined, a hard worker, a competitor, an overachiever,
a leader, and a true student of the game.

Previously, I wouldn't make any decision without thinking of
you first, even though I realize now that you shouldn't rule my
life, I don't regret our past together.

After I pivoted to Georgetown towards business and entre-
preneurship I never thought that I would suit up for another
basketball game again, but then a year later I got an opportu-
nity to compete again on the club team. It was way less com-
mitment and I appreciated that because I had new goals and
dreams that take precedence. Entrepreneurship and business
are still my top priorities. That is why I chose Georgetown, but
I am grateful that I didn't have to completely shut the door on
you as a result of my choice. As long as I live, you will always
have a special place in my heart.

Yours Truly,

Derron Payne

* * *

Bonus PIVOT Point — Appreciate and respect your original path; it may not be the path you want, but it may be the path you need to steer you in the right direction.

* * *

ACKNOWLEDGEMENTS

First and foremost, I'd like to thank my family; My mom, Dani, my grandmother, and Alan, thank you for being the support system I needed. Dad, we haven't always had the best relationship but I'm grateful that we are working on it, thank you for not missing any of my basketball games before college. I know I had a lot.

Thank you, to all of my interviewees. Thank you all for taking the time out of your busy schedules to share your stories with me. Regardless or not if your story made it into the book, every single interview influenced my writing.

Thank you to my best friends Cedric, Engy, and Michael Abi-Habib for always being there for me. I appreciate you more than you know.

Thank you to my brothers from back home, Ced also falls into this category along-side Siree, Julien, and Brad. You guys are some of my closest friends whom have always kept me grounded.

Thank you to my Georgetown family and my closest friends on campus, Michael, John, Edward, Emmanuel, Vikash, Manny, Naomi, Ryan, Dan, and so many more.

Thank you to Jerome, my first co-founder and a huge inspiration.

Thank you to my Cambridge Family, especially Caitlyn and Sophie.

Thank you to all of my mentors Jimmy Lynn, Febin Bellamy, George Repic, Katie Lynch, Hannah Lowney, Fiona, and many more, you all have inspired me so much more than you know.

Thank you to all of my mentees.

Thank you to Eric Koester for inspiring me to write a book. Thank you to Brian Bies, Leila Summers and the entire team who helped me get to the finish line. Thank you to Heather Gomez who remained patient and was supportive of me through the entire process.

I'd like to also thank everyone who pre-ordered my book. Your financial support made this book and it's publication possible. I'd like to take a moment to individually thank everyone who pre-ordered my book:

Eric Koester, Charles R. Hajjar, Daniel Baldwin, Keith Christian Risbrooke, Donna Fyfe, Sherman Fyfe, Kelly Membreno Berrios, Michael Abi-Habib, Joe Delaney, Dani Payne, Bserat Ghebremicael, Juwaun Cooper Muhammad, Amanuel Ghebremicael, Naomi Dukaye, Julian Davis, Percival Atwell, Yahkiney Lynch, John Jenkins Jr., Andres Castro, Darryl Payne, Khadija Risbrooke, Amanda and Cortes Family, Sinclaire Jones, Athalie Harry, Janelle Lowe, Alan Harry, Dorcas Saka, Mia Harvey

I'd like to especially thank the people who invested a higher contribution towards my publishing by ordering multiple copies of my book.

With special thanks to:
Rachel Fyfe
Caitlyn Wiley
Laura G Clark

Thank you to everyone. Your financial support allowed me to transform countless pages of notes and interviews into the book you are about to read.

REFERENCES

Abadi, Mark. 2019. "Mackenzie Bezos Played A Big Role In The Founding Of Amazon And Drove Across The Country With Jeff To Start It". *Business Insider.* https://www. businessinsider.com/how-mackenzie-bezos-met-jeff-bezos-2019-1.

Bezos, Jeff. 2008. "Jeff Bezos - Regret Minimization Framework". *Youtube.* https://www.youtube.com/watch?v=-jwG_qR6XmDQ.

Braun, Adam. 2013. "The Five Phrases That Can Change Your Life: Adam Braun At Tedxcolumbiacollege". *Youtube.* https://www.youtube.com/watch?v=Z8oE2kqVXkk.

Brustein, Darrah. 2015. "9 Entrepreneurs Tell Their Stories Of Pivoting 180 Degrees To Start New Careers". *Entrepreneur.* https://www.entrepreneur.com/article/246965.

Cole, Jermaine. 2013. *Chris Tucker.* Mixtape. Dreamville Records.

Collins, Leslie. 2015. *Bizjournals.Com.* https://www.bizjournals.com/kansascity/news/2015/10/14/alterra-bank-co-founder-switches-gears-to-trucking.html.

Cross, Lindsay. 2019. "Why I Left A Steady Gig To Be A Freelance Writer". *Themuse.Com.* https://www.themuse.com/advice/why-i-left-a-steady-gig-to-be-a-freelance-writer.

"Definition Of PIVOT". 2019. *Merriam-Webster.Com.* https://www.merriam-webster.com/dictionary/pivot.

Fiegerman, Seth. 2017. "Twitter Officially Shuts Down Vine". *Cnnmoney.* https://money.cnn.com/2017/01/17/technology/vine-shuts-down/index.html.

Freeman, Abigail. 2019. "For Jason Nash, Life Is One Long Youtube Video". https://www.bostonglobe.com/business/2019/01/21/jason-nash-has-turned-fun-into-profession/FbCmhzKcC23QQK6gpppPRM/story.html.

Greenawald, Erin. 2019. "A Truly Noble Experiment: Leaving Finance To Open A Rum Distillery". *Themuse.Com.* https://www.themuse.com/advice/a-truly-noble-experiment-leaving-finance-to-open-a-rum-distillery.

Jong, Anneke. 2019. "Career Remix: Why The Jane Doze Quit Their Jobs To Take The Stage". *Themuse.Com.* https://www.themuse.com/advice/career-remix-why-the-jane-doze-quit-their-jobs-to-take-the-stage.

Rayess, Randy. 2019. *Techcrunch.* https://techcrunch.com/author/randy-rayess/.

Siu, Eric. 2019. "How Miss Nevada Lisa Song Built A \$2M/Year Alcohol-Infused Cupcake Empire". Podcast. *Growth Everywhere Podcast.*

Smith, Will. 2019. "How I Became The Fresh Prince Of Bel-Air | STORYTIME". *Youtube.* https://www.youtube.com/watch?v=y_WoOYybCro.

"Vlog Squad - The Shorty Awards". 2019. *Shortyawards.Com.* https://shortyawards.com/10th/vlog-squad.

CPSIA information can be obtained
at www.ICGtesting.com
Printed in the USA
LVHW081428300719
625862LV00022B/456/P